Spouse, Parent, Worker

Spouse, Parent, Worker

On Gender and Multiple Roles

Edited by Faye J. Crosby

Yale University Press   New Haven and London

Designed by Sally Harris
and set in Zapf International type by Lettick Typografic, Inc.
Printed in the United States of America by
Vail-Ballou Press, Binghamton, N.Y.

Library of Congress Cataloging-in-Publication Data

Spouse, parent, worker.

   Includes index.
   1. Sex roles—United States. 2. Role conflict.
3. Wives—Employment—United States. I. Crosby, Faye J., 1947–
HQ1075.5.U6S66 1987   305.3   86-26695
ISBN 0–300–03843–7 (alk. paper)

The paper in this book meets the guidelines for
permanence and durability of the Committee on
Production Guidelines for Book Longevity
of the Council on Library Resources.

10 9 8 7 6 5 4 3 2 1

For
Andrée Cohen Newman and Robert Andrews Newman,
with love and admiration

Contents

Preface

I recently experienced the pleasure and the jolt of coming into contact with the corporeal self of someone whom I had first encountered, years before, in print. The incident led me to ponder reification. In scholarship, and perhaps in all aspects of life, "authorities" tend to evolve into abstractions. Thoughts come to be called concepts, principles, laws, and theories. It begins to seem as if they existed on their own, detached from the people who think them. To meet an admired (or despised) authority in person is to tamper with the illusion of abstract truth. Perhaps this is why the experience is so often emotionally charged.

But authorities are people. Scholars live lives, have feelings, hold values. Neither we nor our theories can escape our collective and personal histories. Students display a tendency to ignore the humanity of academic sources, preferring instead to search the printed page for Truth. In our studies, we seem to wish that the sound of the proverbial tree in the forest did not depend on the acuity of the listening ear. We cajole ourselves into thinking that facts can speak for themselves.

I, for one, have yet to meet a talking fact. Scholars shape facts. Mainstream social scientists today seem most comfortable with an image of themselves as impartial judges of truth or even as data-processing machines. Feminists and other constructionist social scientists, in contrast, seem less threatened than the conservatives by the view of themselves as attorneys arguing a case (Gergen, 1985; Unger, 1986). We can recognize the place of advocacy in scholarly debate by acknowledging the importance of points of view. Advocacy does not invalidate scholarship; it is not dishonest. Values, openly acknowledged, need not impair clear thinking. On the contrary, the muddle results from the pretension that social science can be value-free (Buss, 1975, 1978; Kaplan, 1964).

What are the values that underlie this book on gender and role combinations? The contributors represent a variety of disciplines and research traditions, but they share a similar basic orientation toward the study of roles in the lives of women and men. We all use as a starting point the notion that life opportunities in our society are not equally available to women and men. Our society has made it difficult for women to combine domesticity and participation in the paid labor force. Society is changing now, but the old ways die hard.

The central working assumption of the book, subject to revision on the basis of empirical evidence, has its roots in the existing social scientific literature on role combinations. In the early 1970s a spate of articles and books appeared concerning role combination and women. Among the most influential and insightful of the initial empirical studies were those of the Rapoports (1969, 1971), Bailyn (1970), Epstein (1970, 1971), and Poloma and Garland (1971). These early studies relied on the language of role theory, especially as developed by Robert Merton (1957), and they all told essentially the same tale: wives accommodated their careers and career aspirations to the employment and domestic needs of their husbands. No matter what their employment situation, the women retained full responsibility for their children and the household. Generally, too, women curtailed their occupational investments rather placidly and happily. This meant that men derived only benefits from marriage and from family life; women too reaped advantages from marriage and family, but unlike men they also paid a steep price.

The incompatability of domesticity and career, argued Coser and Rokoff (1971) in a brilliant conceptual piece that appeared at about the same time as the first burst of empirical studies, was more the product of cultural convention than the inevitable consequence of biology. They noted that men systematically exclude married women from professional work on the ground that no one could simultaneously sustain a full commitment to an occupational organization and to family management. Who is the "no one" in question? *Women*, said Coser and Rokoff—for the employed man is routinely expected also to be a "family man." The claim is made, they point out, that a person's deep commitment to any organization—as evidenced by having prestige, being visible, and being relatively irreplaceable—is jeopardized if he or she is committed to another organization as well. The illogic of this point of view is revealed by Coser's and Rokoff's further observations about gender asymmetry. Men are encouraged to perform and are rewarded for performing the same behavior that is labeled problematic in women. An academic department, for example, disapproves of a woman who cancels classes to attend to her family but applauds a male professor who cancels classes to present a paper at a meeting or to manage the affairs of some organization of which he is an officer. In both instances the person fails to meet the needs of one organization in order to care for those of another.

If the reasons put forward to exclude women from professional life seem far from satisfactory, why are women excluded? The real reason that professional work and family cannot mix for women in our culture, according to Coser and Rokoff, is that a married woman is supposed to derive her status in the world from her husband. By engaging in a career of her own, the woman automatically develops an independent status and thereby threatens the social order.

The discrepancy between culturally accepted myths and underlying reality, so neatly described by these and a number of other sociologists, also became salient in the research, largely by psychologists, concerning working mothers. In 1975 Hoffman and Nye published their influential book on the employed mother. Their work and subsequent studies (for example, Scarr, 1984) have shown beyond a doubt that maternal employment does not harm children. It was once common for developmental psychologists (for example, Bowlby, 1951, 1969) to discuss "maternal deprivation" (as often as not, they mentioned the less pejorative-sounding "paternal absence" in the next breath). Today, discourses on "maternal deprivation" as a result of the mother's employment have largely vanished from the scholarly literature.

Attentive as it is to gender asymmetries, this book can be seen as a continuation of the scholarly tradition of Merton, Coser and Rokoff, and Hoffman and Nye. But it also departs in significant ways from paths previously taken. The authors represented here no longer question whether women should be in the paid labor force. Occupational involvement is assumed to be as natural and right for women as it is for men. "Should she or shouldn't she?"—the question implicit in much of the research published during the 1970s and early 1980s—has now become "Given that she does and that he does, what are the benefits and what are the costs?"

From the various empirical findings presented here comes a set of straightforward answers. The benefits of role combination for women lie primarily in enhanced self-esteem and well-being. The woman who participates in the paid labor force also gains both interpersonal power and political involvement. Nothing comes free of cost, however. The chief disadvantages of role combination for women appear to be in terms of increased marital stress. Many husbands are reluctant to share the provider role and become disgruntled as their wives show less dependence on them. Men, like women, may benefit psychologically from multiple role occupancy, but they are less likely to experience childcare as pure delight.

This book rephrases the discourse on multiple roles in another way. Just as we do not see the connection between femaleness and employment as automatically problematic, we do not take as self-evident the connection between femaleness and parenthood (cf. Parsons, 1954). Rather than ask what happens when a woman adds employment to her other roles, for example, these authors ask: how does each of several roles—especially marriage, motherhood, and employment—singly and in combination affect women and men?

The final distinguishing mark of this book is its emphasis on the nature or quality of roles. By treating women's employment as a given rather than as an unusual occurrence, we are less fascinated than some earlier scholars by the mere *fact* that women work. Whether a woman works for pay seems potentially (although not necessarily) a less useful piece of information than what occupation she works in and whether she enjoys her work. With marriage and parenting, as with employment, we emphasize the *nature* of the roles.

The idea for the conference which led to this collection first occurred to me in May, 1983. Conversations with Carol Tavris and Judith Greisman and support from friends and colleagues at Yale University helped implement my plans. Joseph Gordon and Marion McCollum worked hard on procuring funding, and I gratefully acknowledge support from the Mellon Fund for Visiting Faculty and from the Women in Management interest group at the Yale School of Organization and Management. Alan Wagner, Kay Codish, Nancy Cott, and Judith Brandenburg made available monies from Yale's Psychology Department, the Office of Women in Medicine, Women's Studies, and the Yale College Dean's Office. Thanks too to Phyllis Katz for her generosity to the Psychology Department. Ella Futrell, Judy Falcigno, Elaine Cox, Roxianne Bertolini, and Jane Olejarczyk helped me prepare for the conference, which took place in May, 1984, attended by 150 people, mostly academics and almost all women. The speakers included most of the contributors to this book as well as Sharon Baucom-Copeland, Veronica Nieva, Chaya Poitrkwski, and Evan Stark. I thank Kathryn Hemker and Elaine Wilson for additional help with the conference. Joseph Allen, Lisa Gornick, Lisa Silberstein, Claire Sokoloff, and Richard Sussman served excellently as moderators and co-directors of the conference. I also want to express my enormous gratitude to Travis, Matthew, and Timothy Crosby and to Edith Hanf and Sara Ohly.

Crucial to the success of the conference was the attention all concerned paid to linking theoretical abstractions and concrete realities. If we spoke of well-being, we spelled out exactly what was meant by the term; when we spoke of women and men, we specified which women and which men. Speakers laid out their evidence and articulated their inferences (as well as their values and assumptions) whenever possible. In the book that has emerged, we have tried to preserve this directness.

A grant from the Pew Memorial Trust to Smith College and funds from the Committee for Faculty Compensation and Development facilitated my work on turning the conference papers into a book. Also instrumental in this accomplishment were Kay Warren, Mark Zanna, Viola Juanera, Linda Platt, Faith Chudnofsky, Louise Glenowicz, Stephanie Jones, and above all Kathy Bartus. And, as always, there has been the sustaining help and good counsel of Gladys Topkis at the Yale University Press.

Thanks to the hard work of so many people, this book represents a significant turning point in the research on multiple roles, breaking with the old assumption that some roles go naturally with one gender or the other. But one of its shortcomings lies in the fact that most of the women and men studied by psychologists and sociologists, including those whose work is presented here, are middle class and white. We cannot fully understand gender and multiple roles until we know much more about role combinations among women and men across the occupational spectrum and especially about minority women and men.

Research is also needed into how women and men can maximize the advantages of the role combinations while minimizing the disadvantages. Now that we have identified the rewards and costs of what the popular press refers to as "the juggling life," we need to devise and test ways for women and men, in all ethnic and occupational groups, to maintain and increase the rewards without increasing the costs. Given the ferment in research on multiple roles, I am optimistic that answers will be found soon. I also believe that they will require continual updating. But it is my hope and my belief that even after the particular "facts" contained in this book have ceased to apply to the world beyond its covers, students will continue to derive pleasure and knowledge from it.

References

Bailyn, L. (1970). Career and family orientations of husbands and wives in relation to marital happiness. *Human Relations*, 23, 97–113.

Bowlby, J. (1951). *Maternal care and mental health*. Geneva: World Health Organization.

————. (1969). *Attachment and loss*, 2 *vols*. New York: Basic Books.

Buss, A. R. (1975). The emerging field of the sociology of psychological knowledge. *American Psychologist*, 30, 988–1002.

————. (1978). The structure of psychological revolutions. *Journal of the History of the Behavioral Sciences*, 14, 57–64.

Coser, R. L., and Rokoff, J. (1971). Women in the occupational world: Social disruption and conflict. *Social Problems*, 18, 535–54.

Epstein, C. (1970). *Women's place: Options and limits in professional careers*. Berkeley: University of California Press.

————. (1971). Law partners and marital partners. *Human Relations*, 24, 549–64.

Gergen, K. J. (1985). The social constructionist movement in modern psychology. *American Psychologist*, 40, 266–75.

Hoffman, L. W., and Nye, F. I. (eds.). (1975). *Working mothers*. San Francisco: Jossey-Bass.

Kaplan, A. (1964). *The conduct of inquiry: Methods for behavioral science*. San Francisco: Chandler.

Merton, R. K. (1957). *Social theory and social structure*. Glencoe, Ill.: Free Press.

Parsons, T. (1954). Age and sex in the social structure of the United States. In T. Parsons (ed.), *Essays in sociological theory*, rev. ed. Glencoe, Ill.: Free Press. Pp.89–103.

Poloma, M. M., and Garland, T. N. (1971). The myth of the egalitarian family: Familial roles and the professionally employed wife. In A. Theodore (ed.), *The professional woman*. Cambridge, Mass.: Schenkman. Pp.741–61.

Rapoport, R., and Rapoport, R. N. (1969). The dual-career family: A variant pattern of social change. *Human Relations*, 22, 3–30.

————. (1971). *Dual career families*. Baltimore: Penguin.

Scarr, S. (1984). *Mother care, other care*. New York: Basic Books.

Unger, R. K., Draper, R. D., and Pendergrass, M. L. (1986). Personal epistemology and personal experience. *Journal of Social Issues*, 42, (2), in press.

I: Gender and Social Roles: An Overview

1

Role Combinations and Role Conflict: Introductory Perspective

Martha R. Fowlkes

The concepts of status and role are time-honored building blocks in the social scientist's construction of society. They allow us to perceive the links between the individual, the social order, and its culture. The relationships of everyday life are intrinsically social. Individuals consistently act and interact according to culturally prescribed understandings of what is appropriate and expected of them. From a multiplicity of positions in society—called statuses and roles by social scientists—come patterned clusters of behaviors and attitudes that connect people in intricate interpersonal networks. Who I am, my identity, is comprised of the various statuses and roles I hold and my enactment of them. But people are not roles, and roles are not static. Society changes as the lives and values of people change, and with these changes come new roles or new definitions of old roles.

Role combination is a given. Even the homeless, who are typically regarded as the most marginal of society's members, engage in multiple roles with peers, with the general public, and with agents of social control. Why, then, a book about role combination, when role combination describes virtually everyone? What is at issue here is not the fact of role combination per se but the number and kinds of roles that are combined by women and men. Depending on one's gender, certain status/role combinations tend to be defined as problematic and are perceived to encompass competing and/or contradictory commitments. Traditionally, social scientists have conformed to prevailing social norms in viewing combined commitments to family and work as antithetical, especially for women. In the segregationist approach to the study of work and family, each role is seen as greedy for

3

time (Coser, 1974) and as requiring drastically different, even mutually exclusive, value systems and capabilities of its participants. Thus barriers have been erected against women's participation in paid work and men's availability at home.

Certain ascribed statuses (for example, black, female) have historically been associated with specific attributes that are contradictory to the expected characteristics for the most favored occupational statuses. This is what Everett Hughes (1944) had in mind when he wrote "Dilemmas and Contradictions of Status." While membership in the female sex or the black race were thought to be inherently at odds with occupational achievement, for white men the ascribed statuses of race and sex have always been consistent with, even facilitative of, successful role performance in the workplace.

The notion that the role systems of family and work (see Pleck, 1977) entail contradictory commitments is related to the social attributes that came to be popularly associated with the biological categories of male and female in the United States during the industrial revolution. As productive functions moved from home to factory, women's family-based productive roles gave way to roles centered predominantly in household management and childcare (Oakley, 1974). An ideology of femininity emerged that not only justified women's exclusion from the workplace but also their subservience to and dependency upon men (Epstein, 1976; Matthaei, 1982). Historians have labeled this ideology the "cult of true womanhood" (Welter, 1966). As expressed in women's magazines, advice books, and religious literature, the cult of true womanhood applied particularly to white women of the middle and upper classes. It deemed women ill-suited by nature to participate in the hard, competitive world of work. A woman's biology enabled her to bear children and implied her natural abilities for childrearing and homemaking activities. The nineteenth-century cultural norms that segregated women's and men's spheres of work also endowed women with a morality superior to that of men and an inferior intellect. The cult of true womanhood glorified motherhood and designated the private world of the home as the most suitable arena for the expression of the female virtues of softness, passivity, and altruism (Harris, 1978).

Biology argued, moreover, against women's intellectual achievement on the grounds that mental activity generally depleted physical health, specifically reproductive vitality. Nineteenth-century medical science held that a woman's overall health was determined by the health of her reproductive system, which in turn was determined by her behavior and activities. Intellectual pursuits were thought to require an expenditure of energy that a body so dominated by the reproductive function could ill afford. Late nineteenth-century arguments against women's education were circular, claiming both the debilitating effects of educational activity on the menstrual cycle and the debilitating effects of the menstrual cycle on the potential for effective academic or professional performance (Walsh, 1977; Ehrenreich, 1979).

The overtly biological justifications for womens' separate and unequal social roles have altered over time. Initially, women were educated on narrowly utilitarian grounds to prepare them for the work as wives, mothers, and teachers that their separate sphere offered them. Such education did little to challenge prevailing assumptions of women's intellectual inferiority (Cott, 1977). By the end of the nineteenth century, however, the first generation of graduates from the Seven Sister colleges provided ample proof that women's capacity for intellectual development was equal to men's. These colleges made no curricular compromise in the name of a special female intellect and were intended to educate women to the highest standard of education available at that time. On the other hand, in most instances this education was embedded in a sociocultural environment designed to preserve female character and to keep students mindful of the family, religious, and community commitments that awaited their attention as refined and disciplined women. Although it broke with traditional ideas about the mental abilities of women, educational innovation was carefully planned to serve traditional female roles—although it did not always succeed in doing so (Horowitz, 1984).

In the twentieth century, and especially since World War II, the cult of true womanhood has been transformed into the "feminine mystique." The feminine mystique defined expectations for middle-class white womanhood: women were to channel their energies and drives for achievement into the highly elaborated role of the suburban housewife. Said Betty Friedan of the idealized image of the housewife: "She was healthy, beautiful, educated, concerned only about her husband, her children, her home. She had found true feminine fulfillment. As a housewife and a mother she was respected as a full and equal partner to man in his world. She was free to choose automobiles, clothes, appliances, supermarkets..." (Friedan, 1963, p. 13). While the feminine mystique may have held women to high standards of performance in their roles as wives and mothers, it—like the cult of true womanhood—effectively limited their options and roles. Women had no access to occupational statuses; the competition in most of the occupational sector remained the province of men. Over time, the wives' roles came to be highly integrated with the requirements of male careers, further limiting women's opportunities for occupational participation (Finch, 1983; Fowlkes, 1980; Papanek, 1973). Whereas a century ago women tended to be considered naturally unfit for participation in the professional workplace, more recently they are likely to be seen as unable to manage the competing demands of family and work in ways that satisfy the expectations for achievement built into each sphere. With the emergence of role definitions of wife and mother that incorporate expectations of very high achievement, women at work are viewed with suspicion. Role conflict becomes a worry, if not a stigma.

The operative definition of role conflict used here is that employed by Merton (1957) and Goode (1960), who emphasize that, as physical beings, individuals have a finite amount of time and energy available with which to engage in successful role performance. According to this view, commitment to multiple roles is likely to lead to either incompatible or excessive role expectations which result in physical and/or mental exhaustion. Peggy Thoits points out in "Negotiating Roles" (chapter 2) that this view of multiple role occupancy as inherently troubled and troublesome is the subject of debate among sociologists and psychologists. To the extent, however, that this is the conceptualization popularly applied to women as they enter the paid labor force in increasing numbers, it constitutes yet another biologically grounded argument for restricting women's occupational participation. Indeed, the notion of role conflict seems to have become the modern analogue of penis-envy, functioning in a similar way to cast doubt on women who work, especially those who combine work and family roles. Once judged unnatural, such role combinations are now more likely to be regarded as too physically and psychologically stressful to manage, and, on that account, possibly not beneficial. In either case, though, women's biology is the limiting factor.

But women do work: of that there is no doubt. For many women the feminine mystique became a luxury they could ill afford; for others it did not deliver on its promise of self-fulfillment. This book thus addresses the problem of role conflict with reference to contemporary patterns of role combinations. The paid employment of women across occupational and class structures has only recently become a prominent feature of American society. On the other hand, for the most part men have always had a connection to family as well as work. That does not mean, of course, that their roles are identical to women's or that these roles have the same effect on or implications for both women and men. For example, any adjustments women make in order to combine family roles and work commitments are likely to require men to adjust or reexamine their family roles as well. For all of these reasons, much of this book concerns women together with or in comparison to men. The contributors affirm the possibility and desirability of multiple role participation by women and men in both the public and private sectors. A recurring theme is that, not the *multiplicity* of roles, but the *paucity* of roles has a deleterious effect on individual well-being. Finally, this book challenges the assumptions that, where women especially are concerned, it is natural and/or beneficial for adult roles to be confined solely to the domestic sphere.

Chapters 2 and 3—Peggy Thoits on "Negotiating Roles" and Cynthia Epstein on "Role Strains and Multiple Successes"—have important theoretical and practical implications. They remind us that social roles are part of an interpersonally negotiated order and discuss how choice and commitment affect the ways that roles are defined and enacted. Thoits suggests that role conflict can be avoided to the extent that structural and normative freedom permit bargaining. She identifies money, education, and social networks as the three major factors that affect the possibility of role bargaining with respect to both the activities required of a role and the values that organize its definition. Epstein puts these ideas to a practical test in her discussion of women lawyers who successfully combine work and family roles. Her work suggests that multiple successes are possible so long as women are willing to let go of family-based roles as an indicator of personal achievement and to find ways of modifying, sharing, or purchasing the work traditionally associated with those roles. Epstein further suggests that a woman's willingness—indeed, her ability—to change depends on the encouragement and tolerance of those around her.

Part II examines the qualitative dimensions of role combination and their effects on both individuals and relationships between individuals. Abigail Stewart and Janet Malley find that role combination in and of itself is neither beneficial nor detrimental to a women's physical or psychological health (chapter 4). It is, rather, the balance or pattern of agentic and communal orientations reflected in role combination that facilitates emotional and physical health. The connection between quality of life and role quality is further explored by Grace Baruch and Rosalind Barnett, who demonstrate that women's well-being is related to the quality of their role experiences (chapter 5).

The quality of women's role experiences, however, should not be confused with equality of roles between women and men. In their analysis of "Marital Influence Levels and Symptomatology" (chapter 6), Janice Steil and Beth Turetsky show that the higher a wife's pay and the greater the perceived importance of her job, the more equitable the arrangements between the husband and wife for domestic decision making and management. But the link between occupational resources and marital influence does not carry over into childcare, which remains the responsibility of wives. According to Barnett and Baruch, asymmetrical childcare arrangements sustain husbands' marital satisfaction: that is, the more time a wife spends in childcare relative to her husband, the happier he is (chapter 7). Interestingly, this responsibility for childcare is no more problematic for employed women than for full-time homemakers, raising again the larger question of how women's achievement-based needs are met. The woman whose expression of achievement is confined solely to domestic roles will presumably require more recognition of her accomplishments at home than the employed woman whose need for recognition can be satisfied in the workplace.

Robert Weiss's discussion suggests an additional factor. In "Men and Their Wives' Work" (chapter 8), he shows that from a husband's point of view the successful two-career family is one that accommodates rather than alters the asymmetry of the traditional sex-typed division of domestic labor. Men's reactions, as documented by Weiss, probably relate to the ways that men's and women's traditional domestic responsibilities are different and differently evaluated. The woman who adds paid employment to her domestic responsibilities is more likely to see herself and to be seen as "multiply successful." The generally favorable designation of "superwoman" may serve as both an incentive and a reward for women's role combination. In contrast, a man's status is not enhanced if he engages in routine domestic work. To the extent that he does, his traditional family-based status as breadwinner and protector may be obscured. It is the old tomboy and sissy phenomenon: women's status is appreciated by doing the things that men do, and men's status is diminished if they do the things that women do.

The wider social patterns associated with men's and women's role combinations are addressed in part III. In general, people who have more roles are happier than those with fewer roles. Walter Gove and Carol Zeiss, writing on "Multiple Roles and Happiness" (chapter 9), identify gender differences in the meaning attached to various roles. They find that women continue to assign high priority to the quality of their personal relationships alongside whatever work commitments they may have. Lerita Coleman, Toni Antonucci, and Pamela Adelmann, in "Role Involvement, Gender, and Well-being" (chapter 10), underscore the especially positive contribution of the work role to the mental and physical health of both men and women at midlife, when issues of personal identity and individual accomplishment become important. Lois Verbrugge augments this discussion by distinguishing further between roles and role burdens as predictors of health (chapter 11). For both men and women plentiful role responsibility is linked to good health.

Finally, we see that patterns of role participation have political implications as well. Patricia Gurin concludes the book with an incisive analysis of the "Political Implications of Women's Statuses" (chapter 12). She identifies the structural properties of women's statuses as paid workers and homemakers and the effect of those, in turn, on women's existence in the public sphere. She demonstrates that the status of paid worker (and to a lesser extent the status of nontraditional community participant) is consistently related to the formation of gender consciousness and participation in electoral politics.

By extension, then, insofar as the notion of role conflict is invoked by both women and men to justify women's exclusion from the paid labor force, it serves to perpetuate existing patterns of occupational sex segregation together with sex discrimination. Gurin's work makes clear that women whose role commitments confine them to the private sphere tend to take traditional sex roles for granted. Home-based women also have far less opportunity than employed women to perceive gender as a basis for categorical treatment. Role combination in women leads less to role conflict than to awareness of and opposition to restriction to low-quality roles. This book leaves no doubt as to the feasibility of the combination of public and private statuses. And when quality roles are involved, quality rewards result: role combination makes men and women alike healthier, wealthier, and (politically) wise.

References

Coser, L. (1974). *Greedy institutions: Patterns of undivided commitment*. New York: Free Press.

Cott, N. (1977). *The bonds of true womanhood: Women's sphere in New England, 1780–1835*. New Haven: Yale University Press.

Ehrenreich, B. and English, D. (1979). *For her own good: 150 years of the experts' advice to women*. Garden City, N.Y.: Anchor Books.

Epstein, C. (1976). Industrialization and femininity: A case study of nineteenth-century New England. *Social Problems*, 23, 539–57.

Finch, J. (1983). *Married to the job: Wives' incorporation in men's work*. London: George Allen and Unwin.

Fowlkes, M. R. (1980). *Behind every successful man: Wives of medicine and academe*. New York: Columbia University Press.

Freidan, B. (1963). *The feminine mystique*. New York: Dell.

Goode, W. J. (1960). A theory of role strain. *American Sociological Review*, 25, 483–96.

Harris, B. J. (1978). *Beyond her sphere: Women and the professions in American history*. Westport, Conn.: Greenwood Press.

Horowitz, H. L. (1984). *Alma mater: Design and experience in the women's colleges from their nineteenth-century beginnings to the 1930s*. New York: Knopf.

Hughes, E. C. (1945). Dilemmas and contradictions of status. *American Journal of Sociology*, 50, 353–59.

Matthaei, J. (1982). *An economic history of women in America*. New York: Schocken.

Merton, R. K. (1957). *Social theory and social structure*. Glencoe, Ill.: Free Press.

Oakley, A. (1974). *Woman's work: The housewife past and present*. New York: Random House.

Papanek, H. (1973). Men, women and work: Reflections on the two-person career. In Joan Huber (ed.), *Changing women in a changing society*. Chicago: University of Chicago Press.

Pleck, J. H. (1977). The work-family role system. *Social Problems*, 24, 417–27.

Walsh, M. R. (1977). *Doctors wanted: No women need apply. Sexual barriers in the medical profession, 1835–1975*. New Haven: Yale University Press.

Welter, B. (1966). The cult of true womanhood, 1820–1860. *American Quarterly* (Summer, pt.1), 151–74.

2

Negotiating Roles

Peggy A. Thoits

In our attempts to understand the relationships between gender, roles, and mental health, social scientists debate the consequences for women and men of occupying the positions of spouse, parent, and paid worker. Some psychologists and sociologists have focused on the negative effects of multiple role occupancy, while others have argued for the positive effects of combining various roles. The empirical evidence provides unqualified support for neither side in the controversy.

The time has come to move beyond the original question of whether multiple roles help or hinder psychological well-being. After reviewing the arguments and evidence about the effects of multiple role occupancy, this chapter considers the conditions under which the benefits of multiple roles outweigh the costs. My argument turns on the assumption that roles are reciprocal—that it takes two to make a role. From this simple but important observation follow further observations about conflict and role bargaining. I conclude with speculation about role innovation.

Controversy and Evidence

Scholars have long associated multiple role occupancy with harmful effects upon the individual. The reasoning has been that, the more roles one holds, the more likely it is that one will experience incompatible expectations (role conflict) and/or too many demands upon one's limited time and energy (role strain or overload) (Merton, 1957; Goode, 1960; Coser, 1974). The experience of interrole conflict and role strain, in turn, is assumed to cause psychological distress and physical exhaustion. In short, multiple roles have been considered potential sources of stress, which can increase one's risk of psychological and/or physical disorder.

11

Some theorists emphasize the techniques that individuals can use to reduce role conflict and strain (Goode, 1960; Merton, 1957). For example, the individual can abandon one or more roles; she can segregate roles in time and space (to avoid having to choose between incompatible demands); she can assign priority to roles (to justify withholding time and energy from some and not others); and so on. However, situational contingencies may prevent the use of such techniques. For example, a single parent may not be able to relinquish employment, lest she jeopardize her economic survival. When such contingencies exist, multiple role demands cannot be avoided, and stress is likely to be experienced.

This view of the potentially harmful consequences of multiple roles, I believe, is grounded in an "oversocialized" and deterministic conception of human beings (Wrong, 1961), deriving in part from Parsonian theory (Parsons, 1951). Underlying Parsonian theory is the assumption that individuals are motivated to conform to role expectations—in fact, that they internalize those expectations—so that incompatible or burdensome expectations create serious personal dilemmas. Alternatively, theorists have assumed that people conform to role expectations in order to avoid sanctions and gain rewards. Here, pressures for conformity are imposed from without rather than from within. Regardless of the specific assumption regarding the origins of pressures to conform, the traditional view is that conformity to social role expectations is desired by or desirable to the individual, so that incompatible or overwhelming demands produce harmful psychological and physical health outcomes.

Obviously, as several critics have pointed out, the oversocialized, deterministic view of human nature is one-sided (Wrong, 1961; Berger, 1963; Berger and Luckmann, 1966; Stryker and Statham, 1983). Human beings are not just robots programmed by society. They are also willful actors, capable of choosing nonconformity and altering social structure if they so wish. The prevalence of deviant behavior and participation in social movements attest to the limitations of the oversocialized view of human beings. The oversocialized conception errs further in its view of role requirements themselves. Role expectations are not as clear, consensual, rigid, and monolithic as an oversocialized approach implicitly assumes. Critics have pointed out that within the very broad constraints imposed by social structure and normative expectations lie enormous possibilities for negotation, compromise, and innovation. Individuals can construct their own realities to a surprising extent (Berger and Luckmann, 1966). Although "reality construction" theorists may exaggerate the degree to which everyday life is produced by moment-to-moment negotiation, their alternative view serves as a useful reminder that individuals can take an active part in shaping the structure and rewards of their lives. From the constructionist perspective, then, one can argue that multiple roles can be manipulated to yield greater net personal benefit than harm.

Recently, a number of sociologists have developed this theme. For example, Sam Sieber (1974) has pointed out that the privileges, resources, and rewards provided by multiple roles can be parlayed into even more privileges, resources, and rewards. Resources provided in one set of role activities can be used to meet obligations in other role domains: social contacts and technical knowledge acquired in the paid labor market can, for example, be used to the advantage of the family. Such expandable "capital" makes the person more valuable to other role partners. Multiple roles also provide legitimate excuses for failing to meet normal obligations in any one role—the competing demands of other roles can be cited. Finally, multiple roles can buffer the individual against the consequences of role failure or role loss. People who have other involvements may experience less psychological trauma when things go badly in a given role than do people who lack alternative commitments.

The sheer number of roles possessed may also provide gratification and security, increasing self-esteem and a sense of purpose in life (Gove, 1972; Thoits, 1983). Walter Gove has long argued that gender differences in mental health are due in part to the number of roles held by men and women (Gove, 1972; Gove and Tudor, 1973). He has argued from a "beneficial effects" point of view that men generally hold three major roles (husband, father, wage earner) while women traditionally have occupied only two (wife, mother)—therefore, men would be expected to be in better mental health than women.

Gove also qualifies his hypothesis with respect to employed women in light of the special nature of their roles. He suggests that when women hold three roles (wife, mother, wage earner), they are handicapped by a variety of problems: their jobs are intrinsically and financially less rewarding, they bear the major responsibility for childcare and housework despite their employment, and, one might add, they are more likely to experience conflict between childrearing and occupational expectations. Thus, although multiple role occupancy generally is beneficial, according to Gove, it creates greater role strain and conflict for women than for men.

In short, two conflicting views of multiple role occupancy are currently available. According to one, multiple roles are believed to be ultimately harmful to the individual. According to the other, multiple roles are believed to be potentially beneficial. What does the empirical literature show?

Table 2.1: Summary of Studies of Distress Resulting from Multiple Roles

Author	Distress measure	Housewives compared to employed wives	Employed wives compared to employed husbands	Housewives compared to employed husbands	Presence, number and/or ages of children controlled
Pearlin (1975)	Depression	Housewives = Employed Wives	NA	NA	No
Newberry, Weissmann, and Myers (1979)	Disorder (SAD-S)	Housewives = Employed Wives	NA	NA	No
Rosenfield (1980)	Depression	Housewives > Employed Wives	Employed Wives = Employed Husbands[†]	Housewives > Employed Husbands	No
Roberts and O'Keefe (1981)	Depression	Housewives = Employed Wives	Employed Wives > Employed Husbands	Housewives > Employed Husbands	No
Cleary and Mechanic (1983)	Depression	Housewives = Employed Wives	Employed Wives > Employed Husbands.	Housewives > Employed Husbands	No
Radloff (1975)	Depression	Housewives = Employed Wives	Employed Wives > Employed Husbands	Housewives > Employed Husbands	Yes
Gove and Geerken (1977)	Distress	Housewives > Employed Wives	Employed Wives > Employed Husbands	Housewives > Employed Husbands	Yes
Aneshensel, Frerichs, and Clark (1981)	Depression	Housewives = Employed Wives	Employed Wives > Employed Husbands	Housewives > Employed Husbands	Yes
Kessler and McRae (1982)	Distress	Housewives > Employed Wives	NA	NA	Yes
Gore and Mangione (1983)	Depression	Housewives > Employed Wives	Employed Wives = Employed Husbands	Housewives > Employed Husbands	Yes
Gore and Mangione (1983)	Distress	Housewives = Employed Wives	Employed Wives > Employed Husbands	Housewives > Employed Husbands	Yes
Ross, Mirowsky, and Ulbrich (1983a)	Distress	Housewives > Employed Wives	NA	NA	Yes

Totals:
5 studies   Housewives > Employed Wives
7 studies   Housewives = Employed Wives
6 studies   Employed Wives > Employed Husbands
2 studies   Employed Wives = Employed Husbands
8 studies   Housewives > Employed Husbands

[†] Husbands whose wives are employed exhibit greater distress than their wives do.

Table 2.1 summarizes a number of studies. Five report greater distress among housewives than among employed wives (consistent with the "beneficial effects" view), but seven studies report no differences between these two groups of women. When the presence, number, and/or ages of children are controlled, again mixed findings are obtained. Four studies report greater distress among housewives compared to employed wives, while three report no differences between these two groups.

More consistent findings are obtained when employed wives are compared to employed husbands. Six studies report higher distress among employed wives (consistent with Gove's predictions), while two studies find no differences between these two groups. When the effects of children are controlled for, the results are the same. In four studies, employed mothers' distress exceeds that of fathers; one study reports no differences between working mothers and fathers. Finally, perfect consistency is revealed when housewives are compared to husbands. In eight studies that make this comparison, regardless of the parental status of respondents, the distress of housewives exceeds that of husbands.

Clearly, a pure "harmful effects" hypothesis is not supported by these studies. This hypothesis would predict the greatest distress among employed married fathers and mothers, who hold three major roles. But employed married fathers and sometimes employed married mothers instead appear to benefit psychologically from their multiple roles as compared to housewives, who hold only two roles. A pure "beneficial effects" hypothesis also is not supported. It would predict that employed married fathers and mothers would have the least distress of all the groups, again because these individuals hold three major roles. But, although employed married fathers have the lowest distress as predicted, employed married mothers are less clearly benefited by their multiple roles. Instead, they usually exhibit higher distress levels than their male counterparts and often report distress levels equivalent to those of housewives.

Several researchers have suggested that the discrepancies in the findings across studies may be due to historical change (Gore and Mangione, 1983; Ross, Mirowsky, and Huber, 1983b; Kessler and McRae, 1982). More women have entered the paid labor force over the past forty years, and gender-role attitudes have changed substantially (Thorton, Alwin, and Camburn, 1983). Differing proportions of traditional, "transitional," and "new parallel" marriages (see Ross, Mirowsky, and Huber, 1983b) may have been represented in the studies. And different marital patterns may be responsible for contradictory findings in earlier research.

Catherine Ross and her colleagues (1983b) have recently demonstrated that, when one stratifies a sample by type of marriage (traditional, transitional, or parallel), very different patterns of psychological distress emerge for men and women who hold multiple roles. They report the lowest distress levels among husbands and wives in parallel marriages, marriages in which both husband and wife are employed, both prefer the wife to be employed, and both share the housework and childcare. The greatest gender differences in distress, and the greatest distress scores overall, occur in transitional marriages where the wife is reluctantly employed and where the housework and childcare remain her primary responsibility. In these marriages, husbands are more distressed than their wives. Wives are more distressed than their husbands when they prefer employment but the husband does not share housework or childcare. Finally, in traditional marriages, where the wife does not work outside the home, this situation is preferred, and the husband does not contribute to household labor or childcare, wives are still more distressed than their husbands—but both show lower overall distress than spouses in transitional arrangements. In short, discrepancies between husbands' and wives' distress states can be attributed in large part to the structure of their role obligations and the degree to which the couple's actual structures are desired.

Contingencies

The interesting question, then, is not whether the "harmful effects" view or the "beneficial effects" view of multiple roles is more valid, but *under what conditions* will the costs of multiple roles outweigh their benefits? I begin to answer the question by noting a commonplace but crucial aspect of roles that is often overlooked theoretically. Roles are reciprocal. That is, it takes a minimum of two to make a role. Roles are relationships between people—patterned (normative) exchanges of behavior. Furthermore, for role relationships to proceed smoothly, we must be able to "take the role of the other"—that is, we must be able to anticipate accurately and to respond in advance to another's expectations.

Role-taking abilities rest upon shared meanings or understandings (Stryker and Statham, 1983). How I perceive myself in relation to you must be congruent with how you perceive yourself in relation to me in order for us to proceed easily and smoothly in our actions toward one another. In other words, self-definitions in terms of roles must be reciprocal and congruent. And not only self-definitions but behavioral expectations must be reciprocal for smooth interaction. If we mutually define ourselves as friends, but I expect friends never to criticize me while you believe that a major function of friendship is critical feedback, then we have a set of incongruent expectations that will cause us a good deal of trouble. Similarly, if a wife expects her husband to share housework and childcare and the husband views these activities as her responsibility, then these nonreciprocal expectations will generate serious interpersonal conflict, or at least resentful adjustment on the part of one spouse (usually the less powerful one). In short, role conflict and role strain are types of incongruence between the self-definitions and mutual expectations of two or more role partners (Stryker and Statham, 1983).

In a static society, congruent expectations may occur because of widespread and unchanging understandings about the nature of reality. In fluid societies, shared meanings can also result from implicit or explicit negotiation between two people—that is, from interpersonal bargaining. Even in very fluid societies, however, broad structural arrangements and the degree of social consensus regarding the content or shape of particular role relationships constrain the types of bargains struck. For example, the scarcity and expense of childcare facilities is a structural arrangement limiting the kinds of role bargains that husbands and wives can strike with one another if both work. And the degree to which society confers offensive labels on husbands who clean house and care for children will also limit the kinds of bargains that can be made. In short, for those with nonreciprocal, incongruent expectations, *role conflict or role strain will remain high to the extent that flexibility in bargaining is constrained*, where flexibility depends upon the range of possible structural arrangements and the degree of social consensus regarding particular role expectations. It is not, then, the number of roles that causes problems, but rather the degree to which interpersonal renegotiation of rights and obligations is constrained when partners' role expectations are incongruent. Among individuals who hold two or more major roles, role conflict and strain will be high in that subset of individuals faced with structural and normative constraints on interpersonal bargaining. Role conflict and overload will be low in the subset of individuals with greater structural and normative freedom from bargaining constraints (Stryker and Statham, 1983).

What factors inhibit or facilitate a person's bargaining power vis-à-vis her role partner? I want to emphasize relative social power between partners and the strength of social consensus regarding role expectations, both within and outside the relationship (Thibaut and Kelley, 1959). In particular, I identify three major factors affecting bargaining: money, education, and social networks.

Money has the most straightforward implications. First of all, it buys freedom from structural constraints. One need not experience overload due to primary responsibilities for housework and childcare if one can hire others to keep house and supervise children. One need not turn down a job offer far from home if one can afford to commute long distances regularly, as one or both members of dual-career couples often do.

Education is relevant not only because it is often linked to money but because it exposes people to a wider array of possible structural arrangements than they might otherwise encounter. I refer here to increased possibilities for new role bargains suggested through reading, travel, and lectures by "experts."

Both education and money broaden and diversify one's social networks. The more one comes in contact with diverse life styles, the more possibilities for innovation are perceived. Others serve as role models, demonstrating how alternative arrangements can be made and maintained. And the more segregated and differentiated one's social networks, the more likely one is to escape sanctions for nonconformity and to find support for attempting alternative patterns of action (Stryker and Statham, 1983).

Money, education, and diverse social networks not only decrease actual or perceived structural constraints on behavior but decrease perceived consensus regarding traditional role expectations as well. Money buys freedom from normative constraints—the nonconforming behavior of the rich is less likely to be sanctioned and more likely to be admired than the unconventional behavior of the poor. Education and diverse social networks also expose one to varying expectations for the same social roles, which in turn can undermine the legitimacy of traditional role scripts. In short, the more money and education one has and the more diverse one's social networks, the less constraining traditional norms will seem.

Because money, education, and social network differentiation are closely associated with—if not direct indicators of—social class, one might reasonably hypothesize that lower-class individuals who hold multiple roles are less likely to be able to negotiate satisfying rearrangements with their role partners and more likely to experience continued role strain and role conflict—and therefore are more likely to exhibit higher levels of psychological distress than middle- and upper-class individuals with the same obligations. Specifically, I expect social class to mediate the relationship between the number of roles held and reported conflict and strain, as well as physical and mental health. Some evidence along these lines is offered by Meile, Johnson, and St. Peter (1976). They report that when age and employment status are controlled, married women who did not finish high school are more likely to be psychologically distressed than wives who had some higher education, which implies that lower-class wives are more vulnerable to the stresses of their multiple obligations.

Within families, because women are so often at a power disadvantage (especially an economic disadvantage) with respect to men, I expect women to be less successful than men in changing structural and normative constraints on their behavior. Some evidence is available in support of these expectations. Ross, Mirowsky, and Huber (1983b) report that the higher the husband's earnings, the less likely he is to share housework and child-care. The higher the wife's earnings, on the other hand, the more likely her husband is to share these responsibilities. Relatedly, but more indirectly, Horowitz (1982) has shown that men and women who are the chief bread-winners of a family report significantly fewer symptoms of psychological distress than individuals who are secondary earners or unemployed. Horo-witz concludes with two propositions which are consistent with the argu-ment made here: "people who occupy powerful roles have fewer symptoms of distress than those who are powerless"; and "deviation from [tradi-tional] sex-role expectations is productive of distress only when the deviant occupies a relatively powerless role" (619–20). In other words, men and women who make a considerable amount of money may be able to nego-tiate more satisfying distributions of rights and obligations with their spouses and children, thereby reducing the strains (if not the conflicts) of managing multiple roles. Men and women whose earnings are secondary or minimal may be unable to redistribute obligations and thus will suffer continued difficulties and dissatisfaction.

Role Innovation

What are the implications of my constructionist viewpoint? Where should we turn our research attention? Where and what will be the likely forms of innovation in interpersonal relationships? To understand the contingencies that govern role conflict, researchers need not only to document the psychological effects for women and men of various com-binations of activities, but also to attend to expectations. We must remem-ber that variables such as the number of roles (spouse, parent, paid worker) are convenient or approximate indicators of other more general, theoretical factors that determine role conflict and strain. Of crucial importance are expectations. Consider the specific role of academic. I may hold only the role of academic (no spouse, no children, no relatives or friends) and still experience role conflict because of the incompatibility of expectations about teaching and research for a person with limited energy and time.

All participants in the social drama hold expectations. Yet we traditionally study individuals' social experience almost entirely from their viewpoints, without reference to the viewpoints of their significant others. Role negotiations and role conflict are produced by two or more people who interact. Individuals and role partners influence and respond to one another. Researchers have begun to move away from the intensely individualistic orientation and ought to continue to do so.

We need also to consider how the expectations and behaviors of specific sets of individuals are shaped by the larger social structure. Interpersonal relationships occur, obviously, within society. Social structural factors condition much—if not all—interpersonal negotiating. Innovation, therefore, will occur differently in different strata of society.

For individuals with financial resources, education, and differentiated support, role bargaining may result from individual initiative. Of course, to the extent that their role partners have benefited from traditional role arrangements (and to the extent that role partners fail to imagine how change could improve their lot) even the privileged will encounter resistance. I expect, for example, that even affluent women succeed in implementing innovations with their children sooner than with their spouses, as children possess fewer financial and social resources with which to resist change.

The possibilities for role negotiation and innovation are more limited for those who lack financial power, education, and network differentiation. Interpersonal changes for such individuals are likely to depend less upon personal initiative than upon structural and normative changes originating externally. Uncontrollable or involuntary events—natural catastrophes, family crises, plant shutdowns—are likely facilitators of role bargaining (Stryker and Statham, 1983). Major events destabilize established patterns of action and sometimes alter power relationships in the family, thus making room for renegotiation. Initially, new arrangements are likely to be viewed as temporary or necessary expedients for coping with new difficulties rather than as permanent role changes (Stryker and Statham, 1983). But behaviors, when routinized, begin to take on a normative power of their own.

In the absence of cataclysmic or dramatic change, normative shifts in the wider society (for example, regarding the acceptability of careers for women and men's obligation to participate in housework) may also help foster role renegotiation. But because these normative changes occur much more slowly, and because one's family and local networks may be resistant to such changes, appeals for altered role patterns on their basis may be unsuccessful in the short run.

As alternative role bargains are struck more and more often between individuals, certain patterns will become prevalent and routinized; subcultures of consensus regarding the legitimacy of these new arrangements will also grow. However, this is a very slow process, as the change is essentially a grass-roots movement, originating at the interpersonal level and generalizing only gradually to the societal level. Moreover, despite the upsets caused by renegotiation with partners, I believe that middle- and upper-class individuals will be benefited more and sooner than lower-class people, as more advantaged persons have greater freedom from structural and normative constraints. In essence, then, I argue that changes in gender-related expectations and new role arrangements will filter down the social ladder, benefiting more privileged men and women in the short run and those less privileged in the long run.

References

Aneshensel, C., Frerichs, R. R., and Clark, V. A. (1981). Family roles and sex differences in depression. *Journal of Health and Social Behavior*, 22, 379–93.

Berger, P. L. (1963). *Invitation to sociology: A humanistic perspective.* Garden City, N. Y.: Doubleday.

Berger, P. L. and Luckmann, R. (1966). *The social construction of reality.* Garden City, N. Y.: Doubleday.

Cleary, P. and Mechanic, D. (1983). Sex differences in psychological distress among married people. *Journal of Health and Social Behavior*, 24, 111–21.

Coser, L., with Coser, R. L. (1974). *Greedy institutions.* New York: Free Press.

Goode, W. J. (1960). A theory of role strain. *American Sociological Review*, 25, 483–96.

Gore, S. and Mangione, T. W. (1983). Social roles, sex roles and psychological distress. *Journal of Health and Social Behavior*, 24, 300–12.

Gove, W. R. (1972). The relationship between sex roles, mental illness, and marital status. *Social Forces*, 51, 34–44.

Gove, W. R., and Geerken, M. R. (1977). The effect of children and employment on the mental health of married men and women. *Social Forces*, 56, 66–76.

Gove, W. R., and Tudor, J. F. (1973). Adult sex roles and mental illness. *American Journal of Sociology*, 78, 50–73.

Horowitz, A. V. (1982). Sex-role expectations, power, and psychological distress. *Sex Roles*, 8, 607–23.

Kessler, R. C., and McRae, J. A., Jr. (1982). The effect of wives' employment on the mental health of married men and women. *American Sociological Review*, 47, 216–27.

Meile, R. L., Johnson, D. R., and St. Peter, L. (1976). Marital role, education, and mental disorder among women: Test of an interaction hypothesis. *Journal of Health and Social Behavior*, 17, 295–301.

Merton, R. K. (1957). *Social theory and social structure*, rev. ed. New York: Free Press.

Newberry, P., Weissman, M. M., and Myers, J. K. (1979). Working wives and housewives: Do they differ in mental status and social adjustment? *American Journal of Orthopsychiatry*, 49, 282–91.

Parsons, T. (1951). *The social system*. Glencoe, Ill.: Free Press.

Pearlin, L. I. (1975). Sex roles and depression. In N. Datan and L. Ginsberg (eds.), *Proceedings of Fourth Life-Span Developmental Psychology Conference: Normative Life Crises*. New York: Academic Press.

Radloff, L. (1975). Sex differences in depression: The effects of occupation and marital status. *Sex Roles*, 1, 249–65.

Roberts, R. E., and O'Keefe, S. J. (1981). Sex differences in depression reexamined. *Journal of Health and Social Behavior*, 22, 394–400.

Rosenfield, S. (1980). Sex differences in depression: Do women always have higher rates? *Journal of Health and Social Behavior*, 21, 33–42.

Ross, C. E., Mirowsky, J., and Ulbrich, P. (1983a). Distress and the traditional female role: A comparison of Mexicans and Anglos. *American Sociological Review*, 48, 567–78.

Ross, C. E., Mirowsky, J., and Huber, J. (1983b). Dividing work, sharing work, and in-between: Marriage patterns and depression. *American Sociological Review*, 48, 809–23.

Sieber, S. (1974). Toward a theory of role accumulation. *American Sociological Review*, 39, 567–78.

Stryker, S., and Statham, A. (1983). Symbolic interaction and role theory. In G. Lindzey and E. Aronsen (eds.), *Handbook of social psychology*, 3d ed. New York: Random House.

Thibaut, J., and Kelley, H. H. (1959). *Social psychology of groups*. New York: Wiley.

Thoits, P. A. (1983). Multiple identities and psychological well-being: A reformulation and test of the social isolation hypothesis. *American Sociological Review*, 48, 174–87.

Thorton, A., Alwin, D. F., and Camburn, D. (1983). Causes and consequences of sex-role attitudes and attitude change. *American Sociological Review*, 48, 211–27.

Wrong, D. H. (1961). The oversocialized conception of man in modern sociology. *American Sociological Review*, 26, 183–93.

3

Multiple Demands and Multiple Roles: The Conditions of Successful Management

Cynthia Fuchs Epstein

Role strain and the distress that accompanies it are topics of concern in both popular culture and academic circles today. Analyses regularly appear that purport to explain why contemporary women find it difficult to combine successful careers with a full domestic life. But there is something curious about these analyses, which, while representing themselves as sympathetic to women, often convey the misogynist message that women cannot "have it all." Certainly this was the message conveyed in *The Wall Street Journal*'s 1984 Managing Motherhood series (see Crosby, 1985); in "A Mother's Choice," a recent cover story in *Newsweek* (Kantrowitz, 1986); and in an article in the *New York Times*, "For Female M.D.'s, Success at a Price" (Brozan, 1986).

The current focus on role strain no doubt results in part from an honest recognition of the difficulties of meeting conflicting demands. But, in my view, it also results from the fact that some people feel threatened by the vitality and productivity of women with accomplishments in different life roles. What appears to threaten is not the idea of women suffering from the overload of work that results from combining disparate tasks, but the vision of women combining their roles as wives and mothers with high-prestige occupational roles. The objection to women "having to do it all" is really an objection to women "having it all." It reflects, therefore, an objection to women experiencing multiple successes.

Not all women handle the demands of multiple life roles with equal ease. What factors most help facilitate the combination of careers and

23

family? In my studies of women lawyers (Epstein, 1971, 1976, 1981) one factor that seems to contribute to the successful combination of multiple life roles is the emotional support of significant others. If a woman is to experience success at work and at home, it appears crucial that those on whom she relies for support encourage her strivings and applaud her accomplishment.

The current analyses of women who successfully combine multiple roles draw on established sociological concepts. One of the contributions of sociology has been the conceptualization of human behavior as clustering in *roles*. According to Robert Merton's framework, roles are attached to statuses that, in turn, are defined as positions in society. A person occupying a status of mother plays a number of roles associated with it, for example, educating and disciplining a child. Society assigns roles to most people of certain age, sex, and race statuses; and people may choose to play roles attached to the statuses they acquire in occupations, politics, and education. *Norms* specify how people ought to behave and sometimes how they ought to think while playing roles. In modern society the number of roles each person plays is apt to be high. Meeting all the obligations attached to these roles may call for more time and energy than most people have. Juggling too many obligations can result in what is called *role strain*.

Whether a person feels stressed or happily busy depends on the combination of roles she or he has. Society makes it easy or hard for the individual to fulfill the expectations attached to different roles. Role strain can result not only from having a large number of roles to play but also from holding a combination of statuses that is not familiar to most people, or of which they do not approve. Robert Merton (1957) and Everett Hughes (1945) have pointed out that acquisition of some roles (attached to statuses) makes acquisition of others easy or difficult. Certain statuses normatively preclude the assumption of others. Priests, for example, are prohibited from acquiring statuses as husband and father. Some statuses—Hughes calls them *master statuses*—facilitate acquisition of other statuses. Thus, fathers tend to become holders of occupational statuses.

Certain statuses are combined more often than others, resulting in normative expectations that they are "right" or "normal" combinations (Epstein, 1970). People tend to assume that combinations that are found infrequently are wrong. In his famous paper "Dilemmas and Contradictions of Status" (1945), Hughes analyzed how black doctors and women engineers could be made to feel awkward by role partners. Patients who respond to a doctor's female status rather than to her professional one, for example, will make her feel uncomfortable.

Continuity and Change

Many people seem to conclude that combination of multiple roles by women is necessarily problematic. How, they ask, can a woman juggle the demands of a career and a full domestic life? This is one of the big questions of the 1980s, just as one big question of the 1970s was whether women could break down the barriers preventing them from obtaining good jobs and real careers. Those who address this question sometimes seem to regard the issue of women balancing disparate activities as new. But through the ages women have juggled their roles as wives and mothers while performing the multitude of duties typical of the premechanized household (Strasser, 1982; Cowan, 1983; Kessler-Harris, 1981). These women raised chickens as well as children; worked in the fields, made soap, preserved food, and cooked for farmhands. Yet all these tasks were considered to be part of the status of housewife.

So the amount of work is not new. Perhaps the combination of domestic tasks and duties in the "public sphere" of the paid economy is new. Perhaps, but probably not. From the beginnings of industrialization, a sizable number of women had to negotiate the demands of statuses at home and away from home. Many of them cared for parents or siblings and did housework while also working in the factories and offices of an industrializing society (Kessler-Harris, 1981). What *is* new is that many middle-class women now work away from home as well as in the home, even when they are responsible for young children. In 1980, for the first time since official records have been kept, labor force participation among women aged twenty-five to twenty-nine did not decline. In the United States, half of the mothers of children under six work in the paid labor force (Waite, 1981:5). Indeed, the fastest-growing sector of the labor force consists of mothers of preschool children. A large proportion of women, futhermore, are assigning high priority to their work, looking to excel and reap the rewards traditionally expected by men (Bussey, 1986; Hymowitz and Schellhardt, 1986). Women hold half the jobs in some professions, such as accounting (Trost, 1986). What is new, then, is not that women combine many different activities, but that they combine domestic roles with activities outside the home. The news is also that women may, perhaps for the first time, become independent—establish statuses that are not contingent on fathers and

husbands. That women are now able to establish independent social statuses presents a challenge to established modes of thought, and challenges
may be experienced as threats.

Until recently people in our society believed that the typical American
woman was incapable of balancing a checkbook or driving a van. Women's
new competence as bank officers and truck drivers thus created resistance
in many people. It felt discordant to them to see women perform tasks that
should be impossible for them (Cowan, 1983). And it felt odd to see women
competing with men.

Professions, like other institutions, typically defend themselves against
threats. That the legal profession defended itself against the inclusion of
women in its ranks was clear from the histories of the hundreds of women
I interviewed who had tried to become lawyers before the 1970s. To become
lawyers, women had to be stronger, more resourceful, and, in general,
more advantaged than men who wanted to enter the occupation. Cultural
messages suggested that women lawyers were poor risks and worth little
investment in training or in the development of careers. Despite high test
scores and good grades, they were only permitted to practice in low-
prestige, low-paying, and low-responsibility specialties. Women were told
they could not handle their roles as wives and mothers and also assume
high-powered legal careers. The tone of the language used to convey this
message was that of "concern," but the consequences proved more helpful
to the men of the profession than to the women. By keeping women from
the realms of finance and policy, the status quo in the professional community was protected.

Women were told to hold back, to moderate their career commitments,
and not to aim for the rewards of occupational activity appropriate for
men—rewards like money and power. At each crossroad in the path toward
attaining credentials, women faced barriers. Interviewers for law schools
and jobs asked them how they would avoid neglecting their husbands and
children. In law school, women were mistreated by male classmates. Sometimes they were told that they were taking the place of a man who needed
the training to be able to have a career and support a family. Sometimes
the hostility was more subtle. Said one Harvard Law School student: "Practically every male student I met wanted to know 'what is a nice girl like
you doing in a place like this?' They would interrupt my studying in the
library to ask inane questions, confident that I couldn't really be seriously
concentrating."

What did this do to the lawyers? They were caught in a bind. Although many became intent on "proving" themselves to be "better than a man," few dared to state openly that they were pursuing prestige, money, and power. They reported that they wanted to accomplish tasks, help people, make only enough money to support themselves, help their family, or provide needed services.

Women who entered male-dominated professions before the 1970s faced disapproval for aiming higher than they "should" and, if their multiple role demands created overload, they could not expect sympathy. In fact, people were often appalled that women took on these "inappropriate" statuses, especially when they acquired the notice and money attached to them.

The virulent resistance of the 1960s to professional women is gone, but many people continue to defend against the idea of women in law and other prestigious spheres of work. The continued overemphasis on role strain among such women both reflects and contributes to continued covert resistance to their occupational success. Role strain does exist, to be sure; but not to the extent nor in the way that analysts inside and outside the academy have claimed.

My interviews with women in the 1970s who held demanding jobs in law, business, and academia gave me a new perspective on the problem of role strain, one also held by other researchers on women who work. As we documented the many problems women faced, we encountered an interesting paradox. The most successful women lawyers I interviewed turned out to have the most to do. In 1980, of the forty-one women partners in Wall Street firms, twenty-seven were married; all but two had children. Of women judges surveyed in 1982, 68 percent had children (Cook, 1982). Jonathan Cole and Harriet Zuckerman (1983) also report that the most successful married women scientists (of whom 74 percent had children) publish more than their single counterparts.

How could it be that the women on the ladder of success, ably competing with men, can coordinate roles as wives and mothers at the same time? What is their state of mind when they do? In my interviews with the women who juggled careers and family, they downplayed the problems of managing. Despite the absence of childcare programs or flexible work schedules, many of my respondents reported that they felt effective and full of life, a feeling that was also reported to me by friends and that I had experienced myself. Some of the most successful women I spoke to told me they did not feel they had any problems. When I asked one woman, who had attained partnership early in a large corporate law firm, about the

problems she faced in reconciling her roles as a Wall Street partner with
three children under the age of twelve, she answered, "No problems," and
then qualified herself: "Well, not no problems, but none I can't deal with."
That sort of answer was common for women at the top, with demanding
jobs and children, who refused to let problems get in the way of what they
wanted.

These women were problem solvers, not problem seekers, and had become as adept at handling multiple roles as at delegating responsibilitiy in
their jobs. Many articulated well-developed tactics for meeting their diverse
obligations, such as "freezing seven blocks of food each Sunday and thaw-
ing one out each night," moving to the city, hiring caterers and interior
decorators, or asking their widowed mothers to move in. Those with children employed quality help, often more than one person, or enlisted school
personnel to take over in the case of emergencies.

If these resourceful women are strangely absent from the pessimistic
accounts of role conflict, so are some more general theoretical and empirical observations. Three observations appear particularly apposite. First,
problems of overload are not limited to women at the occupational apex.
Second, marriage can facilitate as well as impede professional life. Third,
research shows that certain types of employment situations are detrimental
to mental and physical well-being, no matter what the marital or parental
situation of the people who have those jobs. Analysts rarely point out that
the overload problems of working and maintaining private lives are the
same for women no matter what kind of work they do. Through much of
history, there has been little concern for the long hours women worked in
the household or for the difficult employment they have had as factory and
clerical workers. Few people have thought it important to put limits on the
time or effort women spend at those tasks defined as "woman's work."
What seemed important was circumscribing women within a limited number of roles, not restricting the amount of work encompassed by those roles.

Nor do the Cassandras pay much attention to the simple fact that multiple roles may free a person from some of the role obligations attached to
some statuses. Judith Thomas (1983) shows that divorced parents with
joint custody both perform parental roles but, by sharing these roles with
ex-spouses, they have more time to spend on work and other activities. The
notion that more roles create stress is clearly incorrect in this situation.
Multiple roles create permission as well as pressure to compartmentalize,
one of the mechanisms identified by William J. Goode (1960) by which
people reduce role strain. By compartmentalizing their roles women can

escape from the limitless expectations of the "greedy institution" (Coser, 1975) of the family, in which their role obligations follow a kind of Parkinson's Law, expanding to fill the time available (Epstein, 1970).

Among lawyers and other professionals marriage can also reduce role strain. Social scientists have long noted the occurrence of homogamy: like marries like. Close to half the lawyers I interviewed were married to lawyers. Twenty-two lawyer couples (at last count) teach in American law schools on the same faculties. Among lawyer couples, those who do similar work share interests and understand each other's work. Some couples have problems with competitiveness, but in the balance shared occupational status reduces the role-strain problems of lawyer wives. Lawyer husbands, furthermore, provide their wives with contacts and make it easier for them to be accepted in male networks. The husband also helps protect the wife from sexual harassment at the office. Debra Kaufman (1978) has shown that married women academics are more integrated into male networks than their unmarried female colleagues and are more often able to use the contacts they make through these professional networks.

The last blind spot of the doomsayers concerns the data on physical and mental well-being. As women, perhaps more than ever before, have a chance to attain power, authority, and money, warnings are emitted from both scholarly and popular quarters that paid labor may be hazardous to women's mental and physical health, especially if it is combined with domestic duties. The implication is that high-prestige, well-paying, powerful jobs come at an enormous cost. What are the facts? Medical research has now established that those who are most at risk for hypertension and heart disease are individuals who work at jobs where they are permitted to make few decisions and where demands are high—for example, white collar jobs in which employees are ordered about and permitted no reprieve (Karasek, 1979; Karasek et al., 1981; Karasek et al., 1982). While certain work situations create distress, others promote well-being. Joanne Miller, Melvin Kohn, and others have discovered that women and men who work at jobs that encourage self-direction develop the ability to be open, flexible, and intellectually adept. (Miller et al., 1979).

It seems, in short, that women who appear to suffer from role strain may actually be suffering from the negative aspects of one or more of their roles. Rather than creating stress, a full home life can reduce stress by protecting individuals and by allowing them to take a broad view of difficulties at work (Crosby, 1984). There is, in fact, strong evidence that people who are married and have children like their jobs better than single people do (Bersoff and Crosby, 1984; Crosby, 1982).

Not all women combine work and family life with equal success. Among the lawyers I studied, some managed much more easily than others to enjoy simultaneous success at work and at home. What factors differentiate the women who managed well from those who managed poorly? The first impulse is to look for differences in the women's personalities. It is no doubt true that idiosyncratic differences exist and that some women seem to thrive on stress, while others dislike it. Hans Seyle (1956, 1974), a psychologist and stress expert, wrote some time ago that stress can be either negative or positive. Positive stress, for some people, can lead to exhilaration. Many of the women I interviewed enjoyed their demanding jobs and the satisfactions of prestige and power. Their confidence came from becoming accomplished in a respected profession, doing work that many people thought was beyond women's capacity. These women had begun to win cases in court although they had been told that they didn't have "the right stuff" to be courtroom attorneys. They were doing good corporate work despite being told that corporate law was a male field. They had also begun to prove themselves good at finance law. Success at juggling roles further increased these women's confidence. As one lawyer put it: "I feel successful this year because I did what I set out to do, have a baby and still practice law and make some income out of it. As a bonus to that, I succeeded in getting some interesting cases."

The women who seemed to thrive the most on the challenge of managing multiple roles were those who experienced the least guilt about delegating duties at work and at home. Successful women experienced little conflict about using paid help. The higher their rank in the profession, the more adequate help they could obtain. These women did not tend to brood about the amount of time they spent with their children, but rather defined circumscribed times with children as adequate—whether every evening or only weekends. Many of these mothers felt comfortable letting their husbands take on parenting responsibilities that other women tend to guard more jealously. They also seemed aware that there are fads and fashions regarding what is considered quality care for children (or for husbands or lovers). Women with demanding practices often seemed more pragmatic than idealistic.

Ironically, many of the women who worked in feminist law firms tended to think ideologically about a number of matters, including childcare. Lawyers in feminist firms sometimes assessed themselves more harshly as mothers than did the more "practical" attorneys. As a result, the feminist attorneys more often than others found themselves in a quandary over their multiple roles. Why did some women experience guilt and others not?

Personality differences did not appear to be the major determinant of women's ambivalence. What seemed instead to matter crucially for successful role management were the reactions of significant others at home and at work.

Parents often communicate traditional sentiments about their daughters even when they are grown. Some parents unequivocally express either pride or shame about their daughters' professional accomplishment. Others communicate ambivalence. One woman said:

> My mother is a businesswoman. But she resents being one. She says she would much rather have stayed home and had three more children. Her attitude about practicing law was that it was unfeminine and I should get married and have children. I'd never find a husband if I graduated from law school. She says she hates her job, but she is successful at it and really loves it. She functions best on her job, but she will tell you that all she really wanted to do was be a mother and a housewife. Yet she was so proud when I was admitted to the bar. She came into the office full flourish, with her mink coat—the works....She'll talk about "my daughter, the lawyer"—but not in front of me.

Another repeated the theme: "My mother said it was the happiest day of her life when I called her up and told her I wanted to be a lawyer. But my parents worry about me. For a while they were very upset that I seemed to be drifting away from my husband. My father said, 'Don't do it. Quit your job before you ruin your marriage.'" For these women and others, parental ambivalence fuels guilt about professional accomplishment.

Even more consequential than the reactions of parents are the reactions of husbands. Husbands can withhold support for their wives because of competitiveness. A young associate on Wall Street whose husband was an associate in another firm addressed the problem openly in an interview a few years ago. Asked what would happen if she became a partner and he did not, she responded:

> That would be a catastrophe! I would feel rotten about it. We joke about it all of the time. I always say, "Just wait!" And he says, "Terrific, you make partner and I will retire." But, you know, I think it would just kill him. In fact, with that thought in mind, I have often told him that if he wanted to leave and move, even to another city, I would be willing to do that. Just because it is more important for me to have a happy husband.

A law school professor told me of a woman who refused an opportunity to excel in her career to keep peace with her husband.

I know of a lawyer who is married to a man twenty-five years her senior. They both work in the same law office. She had a chance to get out and go to a big, classy firm. He went into a depression, serious depression. They had it out. She convinced him that if she wanted to go she should. But she didn't take the job. She said it was for lots of reasons...the offer wasn't what it should be; the prospects for becoming a partner were not wonderful. But I don't think if the prospects had been any better she would have taken that job. Her husband did not talk to her for two months. They lived in a house with the children and he would not talk to her. He told her the reason. He did not want his wife in a job with more prestige and attention and more money. She was going to be traveling around the country and meeting people and was going to outshine him. He said it was a double standard and he knew it, but he wasn't going to change. He said she knew it when she married him and he was not going to discuss it any more. And he didn't.

Some husbands wanted to support their wives' commitment to work but found it difficult to translate their attitudes into behavior. One young law professor spoke of the course of her marriage, which ended in divorce:

When I met my husband, practically the first conversation we had was "what do you think of working women and smart women and ambitious women?" And he reacted positively to all those things. I had strong ideas then about independence and nobody holding doors for me and that kind of thing. But much later when it fell apart, and it seemed to be falling apart because of the amount of time and energy I was putting into work, I would say things to him like "this should come as no surprise; there was never any deception about who I was...." He answered, "I thought that what you were was what I wanted, but I found I couldn't live with it."

What happens when a woman has the whole-hearted support of her husband? She is freed from a burden of guilt about her professional accomplishments and able to accomplish even more than other women. Typical of high-achieving women with supportive husbands was one who successfully practiced law with her husband in a situation where she outranked him. "I have had the distinct pleasure of hearing my husband discuss the awesome benefits of having his wife as a law partner. He tends to emphasize how his comfort level is increased because of the absolutely unquestioned loyalty that he knows is part of his relationship with his law partner. He also emphasizes his security in working with a known quality and with someone whose abilities and capabilities he has no doubt about."

Good partnerships provide fewer dramatic episodes than the troubled or troubling ones. When people are functioning well as a team, they do not provide noteworthy quotations about their relationships. On the basis of countless conversations with young people across the country, I have come to see that the gloom-and-doom scenerios of the "experts" are vastly exaggerated. Aspiring young professionals appear to be more aware of the problems of multiple commitments to work and home than their older counterparts were. They also appear more prepared to cope. Situations do vary in how stressful they are, and there are times when roles are hard to combine. But the current emphasis on role strain in both academic and popular analyses does not provide an accurate description of reality. People differ in their responses to conditions of multiple demand, and there are considerable differences in perception about highly demanding situations. Some women feel defeated; others exhilarated. Of the utmost importance is the social environment. Cultural norms can make it easier or harder to combine domestic duties and career. The same applies, many times over, to the attitudes of the significant people in a woman's life. The essence of role management is that it is done in conjunction with others. Friends and relatives have to be amenable to the new rules. The successful women I studied had in common one crucial element—the good will and supportiveness of others in their lives on their way to "having it all."

References

Bersoff, D., and Crosby, F. (1984). Job satisfaction and family status. *Personality and Social Psychology Bulletin*, 10, 75–83.

Brozan, N. (1986). For female M. D.'s, success at a price. *The New York Times*, April 16, C-1.

Bussey, J. (1986). The industrial revolution: Women running factories. *The Wall Street Journal: Special Report on the Corporate Woman*. March 24, 14.

Cole J., and Zuckerman, H. (1983). Marriage, family, and women's research performance. Paper presented at American Sociological Association Meeting, New York, New York.

Cook, B. B. (1982). Dual roles of women judges. Paper presented at the Symposium for Women Judges, April 16, Wingspread, Wis.

Coser, R. L. (1975). Stay home little Sheba: On placement, displacement, and social change. *Social Problems*, 22, 470–79.

Cowan, R. S. (1983). *More work for mother*. New York: Basic Books.

Crosby, F. (1982). *Relative deprivation and working women*. New York: Oxford University Press.

———. (1984). Job satisfaction and domestic life. In M. D. Lee and R. N. Kunango (eds.), *Management of work and personal life*. New York: Praeger. 41–60.

———. (1985). Working motherhood and the *Wall Street Journal*. *Working Mother Magazine*, August.

Epstein, C. F. (1970). *Woman's place: Options and limits in professional careers*. Berkeley: University of California Press.

———. (1971). Law partners and marital partners: Strains and solutions in the dual career family enterprise. *Human Relations*, 24, 549–64.

———. (1976). Sex role stereotyping, occupations and social exchange. *Women's Studies*, 3, 185–94.

———. (1981). *Women in law*. New York: Basic Books.

Goode, W. J. (1960). A theory of role strain. *American Sociological Review*, 25, 483–96.

Hughes, E. C. (1945). Dilemmas and contradictions of status. *American Journal of Sociology*, 50, 353–59.

Hymowitz, C., and Schellhardt, T. D. (1986). The glass ceiling: Fighting barriers to the executive suite. *The Wall Street Journal: Special Report on the Corporate Woman*, March 24, 1, 4–5.

Kantrowitz, B. (1986). A mother's choice. *Newsweek*, March 31, 46–51.

Karasek, R. (1979). Job demands, job decision latitude, and mental strain: Implications for job redesign. *Administrative Science Quarterly*, 24, 285–307.

Karasek, R., Baker, D., Marxer, F., Ahlbom, A., and Theorell, T. (1981). Job decision latitude, job demands, and cardiovascular disease: A prospective study of Swedish men. *American Journal of Public Health*, 71, 694–705.

Karasek, R., Theorell, T., Schwartz, J., Pieper, C., and Alfredson, L. (1982). Job, psychological factors, and coronary heart disease. *Advanced Cardiology*, 29, 62–67.

Kaufman, D. (1978). Associational ties in academe: Some male and female differences. *Sex Roles*, 4, 9–12.

Kessler-Harris, A. (1981). *Out to work: A history of wage-earning women in the United States*. New York: Oxford University Press.

Merton, R. K. (1957). *Social theory and social structure*. Glencoe: Free Press.

Miller, J., Schooler, C., Kohn, M., and Miller, K. A. (1979). Women and work: The psychological effects of occupational conditions. *American Journal of Sociology*, 85, 66–94.

Seyle, H. (1956). *The stress of life*. New York: McGraw-Hill.

———. (1974). *Stress without distress*. Philadelphia: Lippincott.

Strasser, S. (1982). *Never done: A history of American housework*. New York: Pantheon.

Thomas, J. (1983). Co-parenting and careers: Divorced mothers discover advantages in dual households. Paper presented at the Eastern Sociological Society, March, Philadelphia, Pa.

Trost, C. (1986). The new majorities: Some traditionally male professions are becoming dominated by women. *The Wall Street Journal: Special Report on the Corporate Woman*, March 24, 15.

Waite, L. (1981). U. S. women at work. *Population Bulletin*, 36, 1–44.

II: Individuals and Their Social Roles

Multiple Regressions and Multiple Roles: A Note for the General Reader

Faye J. Crosby

The chapters in parts II and III refer to procedures common to inferential statistics, most often to multiple regression analysis. The general reader can understand the arguments and the evidence without being familiar with inferential statistics, but for those who want to know the logic behind multiple regression analyses, the following brief guide is offered.

The Principle of Covariation

Imagine that you are researching the connection between role involvement and mental health. You wish to test empirically the proposition that involvement in the worker role is associated with good mental health in women. Your hypothesis states that the greater the involvement, the better the mental health. You find a sample of employed women and you assess, say through a questionnaire, each woman's mental health and her job involvement. Your questionnaire contains twenty questions about job involvement that can be scored quantitatively. Altogether, your Job Involvement Scale runs from 0 (no involvement) to 40 (full involvement). Your Mental Health Scale has many items and runs from 0 (mentally unhealthy) to 100 (mentally healthy).

Correlations

How can you test your hypothesis about an association between mental health and job involvement? You can plot on one graph each woman's mental health score and job involvement score and look for a pattern.

Figure 1 plots data where no pattern exists, and where there is no association between mental health and job involvement. In figure 2, the two variables covary perfectly. Each increase in job involvement is matched by an analogous increment in mental health. Figure 3 presents a more typical situation, in which mental health and job involvement tend to "go together" but are not in perfect synchrony. Generalizing from figure 3, you could conclude that your hypothesis is by and large correct—the more involved a woman is in her job, the healthier she is.

Graphs are informative, but rather clumsy. Social scientists have developed a statistical technique that allows one to summarize in a single number the relationship between two variables. The statistic is called a Pearson's r or correlation coefficient. A correlation coefficient simply tells us the extent to which two variables are yoked so that changes in one score "predict" or are associated with changes in the other. The Pearson's r can vary between $+1.00$ and -1.00. A correlation coefficient of $+1.00$ means that an increase of one unit in a given variable (say job involvement) is, without exception, accompanied by an increase of a given unit in the other variables (say, mental health). A correlation coefficient of -1.00 means that an increase of one unit in a given variable is, without exception, accompanied by a decrease of a given unit in the other variable. When there is no association between two variables, the correlation coefficient is 0.00. The data plotted in figure 2 would have a correlation of $+1.00$, while the data in figure 1 would have a correlation close to zero. The Pearson's r for the data in figure 3 would be about 0.70 or 0.80.

Clearly, you could convince other social scientists about the truth of your hypothesis more efficiently with a statistic like the Pearson's r than with a graph. A correlation coefficient has another benefit: you can use additional statistical formulae to determine whether the degree of covariation you have found between two variables among a given sample of people is likely to have happened by chance or is likely to prove reliable (that is, reproducible in other samples of people). If the covariation between variables is orderly enough and if the sample is large enough, then the additional tests will show that the correlation is *statistically significant*. Statistical significance has, of course, nothing to do with social significance. For all inferential statistics (not just correlations) the convention is to note whether the observed covariations are of the type that occur by chance fewer than five times out of one hundred (denoted by $p < .05$), less than one time in a hundred ($p < .01$), or less than one time in a thousand ($p < .001$).

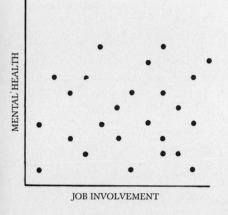

Figure 1

No Correlation

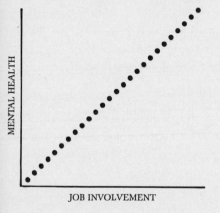

Figure 2

Perfect Positive

Correlation

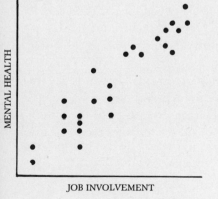

Figure 3

Some Correlation

Regressions

Correlations are, then, quite useful. But they have one big problem: generally speaking, they can only be computed for associations between two variables at a time. What if other factors might also be important? Imagine that I challenge your findings on the association between job involvement and mental health by claiming that mental health is not enhanced so much by job involvement as it is by money. Money and job involvement tend to go together, I claim, and your Job Involvement Scale was really only an indirect measure of earning power.

How could you refute my claim? You could administer an Earning Power Scale along with a Job Involvement Scale and the Mental Health Scale. You could then see whether mental health correlates more strongly (in a specific sample) with job involvement than with money. Or you could divide the women into categories such as "high and low earners" or "high, medium, and low earners" and then calculate the correlation between job involvement and mental health within each category. The second strategy is superior to the first because it allows you to look simultaneously (rather than serially) at different factors.

Matters are manageable, if not perfect, so long as you are dealing with only three variables. But your analysis will quickly become chaotic when I pose further factors (for example, the women's ages, marital situations, family situations) as either alternative explanations or mediating variables. How to create categories (should it be high and low earners or high, middle, and low? is a tripartite division better than a dichotomous one?) presents one problem. Finding enough people to "fill" each category is another.

Enter the multiple regression analysis. This is, in essence, a procedure that allows you to compute correlations between one variable (say, mental health) and many other variables simultaneously. The formulae automatically make adjustments in the correlations between the *criterion variable* (for example, mental health) and any other *predictor variable* (for example, job involvement) that reflect the existence of other predictor variables (say, earning power or age).

A popular variety of multiple regression analysis is known as the hierarchical multiple regression analysis. Hierarchical regressions are designed to consider the associations between predictor variables and the criterion variable in stages. In this analysis, one typically establishes the covariation between the criterion variable (mental health) and a set of mundane predictors (age, salary) first, and then one checks to see if the more theoretically interesting variables (job involvement) add anything to the story.

In sum, while multiple regression analyses are technically sophisticated, they are logically rather simple and elegant. They allow researchers to examine the covariations between a variable of special interest and a number of other different factors. Conceptually, they function like an elaborate set of correlations or, for the visually attuned, like a many-faceted set of scatterplots.

4

Role Combination in Women: Mitigating Agency and Communion

Abigail J. Stewart and Janet E. Malley

It has been widely assumed, both by certain academic groups (such as role theorists) and by the lay public, that it is difficult for women to combine career and family (see, for example, Ibrahim, 1980). However, in recent years evidence has gradually accumulated to suggest that the difficulty involved in role combination has been exaggerated and that its effects are less clear-cut than has been previously assumed (Verbrugge, 1982; Baruch, Barnett and Rivers, 1984; Belle, 1982). For example, Stewart and Salt (1981) found that young women with multiple role involvements showed fewer physical and psychological stress responses when faced with life change than did their counterparts who were involved with fewer roles. Role combination, in that study, was not associated with the level of psychological or physical symptoms women reported. But it did serve as an important intervening variable in predicting women's responses to life changes. Unmarried career women responded to life changes in the way we have come to expect men to: with physical illness. In contrast, housewives responded to life changes in the way we traditionally expect women to: with depression. But the two groups who combined roles (married women with careers and married women with careers and children) both showed no particular negative response to life changes.

We are grateful to our colleagues Nicole B. Barenbaum, Carol E. Franz, and Joseph M. Healy, Jr., for their help in developing the codebook and coding and analyzing the data described in this paper. We are also grateful to Deborah E. Belle, Anne P. Copeland, Daryl Costos, Frances K. Grossman, Hildreth Youkilis Grossman, M. Brinton Lykes, Kathleen M. White, and David G. Winter for quick, thoughtful, and helpful feedback on our earliest version of this paper. Data described here were collected and analyzed with support from the Spencer Foundation and NIMH grant R03MH3902.

Stewart and Salt speculated in their study about why single career women, housewives, and women combining family and job roles differed in their responses to life changes. For example, women in the various groups might differ in the degree to which they controlled or chose their changes. Perhaps single career women felt solely responsible for life changes, and housewives completely responsive to the decisions of others, while the role combination groups felt some control but also some sharing of responsibility and help. Alternatively, perhaps the single career women responded to life changes largely with instrumental, active coping efforts which strained them, thereby falling prey to illnesses, while housewives responded with affective and communicative but noninstrumental responses which heightened their sense of helplessness. Women with mixed roles might have used both response modalities and thus balanced the fatigue deriving from instrumental coping efforts with the emotional support and perspective derived from inactivity and interaction.

Of course, personality or energy differences among the four groups, rather than role combination, might account for the results. To help rule out this possibility, Stewart and Salt pooled the four groups of women and examined, across all groups, the effect of job related changes (including the stress of losing a job or failing to find one) and of family changes (such as deaths, children going to school, moves). Interestingly, across the groups, job changes resulted in physical illness, while family changes resulted in depression. Thus, the two role *arenas*—job and family—seemed to carry different stress risks regardless of the individual's personality or other characteristics.

In this chapter we extend this line of research to data drawn from a heterogeneous sample of recently separated mothers of school-age children. We present case studies and quantitative data in an effort to explore how women with various life structures respond to the stress of marital separation. Our sample of women were all custodial and therefore retaining the parent role, but their employment outside the home varied. Half of the mothers held full-time jobs when they were first interviewed, about six months after they separated from their husbands; and one-quarter held part-time jobs. We also gathered a comparison sample of forty-nine mothers of school-age children who were not getting divorced but who lived in the same neighborhoods as the divorcing mothers and were comparable to them in age, education, length of marriage, and ages and number of children. In line with the results of the previous study, divorcing mothers who did not have jobs outside the home were significantly more depressed than the housewives who were not getting divorced, but they did not experience higher stress. Also in line with previous findings, but more surprising, divorcing mothers who worked full-time showed no higher level of stress symptomatology than working mothers not getting divorced (table 4.1). Thus, the connection between sole occupancy of family roles and depression held up in the sample of divorcing mothers, and the protective function of simultaneous role occupancy also seemed to hold up, even in this highly stressful situation. Why was this so?

Table 4.1: *Depression and Physical Stress Symptoms among Mothers of School-Age Children*

	Score on:			
	Depression		*Stress symptoms*	
Group	N	Mean	N	Mean
Mothers not employed outside the home				
Recently separated	27	14.26	27	35.41
Remaining married	14	4.29	7	29.71
Difference		9.97		5.70
		t = 2.76		t = 1.55
		p < .01		NS
Mothers employed full-time outside the home				
Recently separated	53	13.23	53	35.59
Remaining married	13	8.59	8	31.00
Difference		4.64		4.59
		t = 1.43		t = 1.65
		NS		NS

Note: NS = not significant.

Our review of our own and other researchers' findings led us to suspect that there might indeed be relatively broad, role-linked threats to mental and physical health. Thus, job roles, with their demands for choice, task performance, and efficacy, might carry a general risk of physical illness, while family roles, with their demands for communication, closeness, and caring, might carry a general risk of depression. This reasoning is consistent with that expressed by Bakan in *The Duality of Human Existence* (1966). Bakan explained:

I have adopted the terms "agency" and "communion" to characterize two fundamental modalities in the existence of living forms, agency for the existence of an organism as an individual, and communion for the participation of the individual in some larger organism of which the individual is a part. Agency manifests itself in self-protection, self-assertion, and self-expansion; communion manifests itself in the sense of being at one with other organisms. Agency manifests itself in the formation of separations; communion in the lack of separations. Agency manifests itself in isolation, alienation, and aloneness; communion in contact, openness, and union. Agency manifests itself in the urge to master; communion in noncontractual cooperation. Agency manifests itself in the repression of thought, feeling, and impulse; communion in the lack and removal of repression.(15)

Bakan suggests that "unmitigated agency"—agency without communion—can result in physical illness. Given the results of Stewart and Salt (and others), we think Bakan is right; and we also suspect that "unmitigated communion"—connection and feeling without self-assertion and self-protection—can result in depression. The two trends seem to be neutralized by their simultaneous presence.

It is unlikely, though, that there is a one-to-one correspondence between agency and communion, on the one hand, and work and family roles, on the other. While job roles may be in general highly agentic in their demands, some jobs and some aspects of jobs are clearly communal. Drawing on our own work experiences, it seems clear that talking with students, working in our research group, even collaborating on papers are activities which at least sometimes demand communication, closeness, and caring. But writing, analyzing data at a computer terminal, and balancing the grant accounts all draw more from the realm of task performance, choice, and efficacy. Similarly, in our family lives we could see elements of agency (scheduling doctor's appointments, choosing schools and camps, handling emergencies) and of communion (taking walks, reading stories, and bedtime chats). Different families' lives may be composed of different degrees of agency and communion. Perhaps the important thing is not the presence of the roles per se, but the presence of the two "fundamental modalities" in our lives.

We had few guides in beginning our exploration of the possibility that it is the agentic and communal aspects of family and work roles that matter, not the roles per se. But we began to develop a sense of what we had in mind as we read over transcripts of our interviews with divorcing mothers. Women who emphasized the communal aspects of their work or their family spoke in terms of relationships and connections, of collective actions rather than individual ones, and of a sense of mutual dependence with family members and colleagues. Women who expressed the agentic aspects of their lives emphasized individual initiative, separate tasks and activities, and their own and others' independent spheres of action. Naturally, many women spoke about both aspects of both arenas.

Case Studies

Our first step in exploring agency and communion was to select four women as case studies. We chose them first on the basis of the way they described their jobs and family lives. If a woman described her job or family mainly in terms of collective activity and relationships, we viewed her orientation to that sphere as primarily communal; if she described it in terms of separate tasks and individual responsibilities, we viewed her orientation to it as agentic. We selected four women: two who expressed a communal or agentic orientation in both spheres, and two who expressed opposite mixtures: agentic job and communal family orientation, and agentic family and communal job orientation. These four women, then, represented unmitigated agency, unmitigated communion, and two different blends of the two orientations.

Our questions were: do the women with unmitigated orientations show more strain that those with mixed orientations? Does unmitigated agency seem to result in a different strain than unmitigated communion? If the two unmitigated orientations are most stressful, are they also less stable over time than the two mixed ones? We explored these questions in interviews with the four women, the first only a few months after their separation, and the second one year later. We also examined the women's responses to standard questionnaire measures of mental and physical health. We have changed no essential data about these women, but we have given them fictitious names, make no reference to identifying information, and have altered slightly or concealed some details in order to protect their privacy.

Annette: Communal Orientation to Both Work and Family

The woman we chose whose orientation to both work and family seemed to be predominantly "communal" was in her early thirties, had two children under eight, had been married about ten years, and had been working as a full-time classroom teacher of young children for over a year when we first saw her. Annette described her work situation in the period shortly after the separation as "very supportive"; she also indicated that it was "crazy—that's what it is....I get one free period a day. And usually I either spend it running around talking to teachers, or sometimes I try to relax." She explained that her work involved "group activities" all day, with the ten kids assigned to her, and remarked, "that's really trying. It's exhausting, it really is."

Annette's home life also involved much group activity. After school, she picked her children up from the babysitter and "the children usually found some things to do." Around five, she began getting supper ready, involving both children in the process. After dinner, all three cleaned up together and then all played a game or told a story. Annette expressed great pleasure in being with her children and spent a great deal of time with them on weekends cleaning the house, visiting friends, and doing projects. On Sunday afternoons the children visited their father, and Annette spent a few hours alone.

Overall, Annette experienced the post-separation period as a release. When asked which part of her day was easier after the separation, Annette said getting up in the morning was easier because she was no longer depressed about facing a new day. In contrast, the most difficult part of the day for her was the evening, partly because her husband used to supervise the children while she prepared and cleaned up dinner. Annette described a "typical time when [she] would be feeling this way":

Okay, we get in the house, okay, and the kids are running around and they're bouncing off the walls, so I say, "Okay go play with some toys, I have to get supper ready." I'm starting to get supper ready, Andrea brings all her toys into the kitchen—it's a very tiny, a teeny, teeny kitchen, and I go to go in the refrigerator, and I'm falling over her and Stephen's coming in, and it's like "get out of here and leave me alone. I want to make dinner." I hate that time....I need some time to just be by me. Just to, you know, start at step one and go to step whatever and get it done and not have constant interruptions like that.

It is clear that, at least in the early post-separation period, Annette was relieved to be getting divorced but was finding her day-to-day life pretty stressful. She scored higher than other women in the sample on stress symptoms such as sleep difficulties, anger, and fatigue. She hoped that in the future she would find "a nice guy" and "have a very stable, happy family life with a remarriage....I think I need that kind of one-to-one and that kind of family closeness."

In the second interview a year later, Annette mentioned that she was planning to move in with a man she had recently met and expressed real dissatisfaction with her work life. She said she could now see how people "get burned out very quickly with that kind of job," and she hoped to find an administrative position that still included some student contact. As she put it, she wanted "something that's not so intense....I know I can't take it forever." Moreover, by this time, Annette saw her work and family life as very directly linked: "I have bad days with the kids in school and it really affects my relationship with the kids....It has been a conflict. I have considered getting out because of it. Because of the demand in school...I get really depressed...I really get drained. And sometimes I ask myself, 'Why am I doing this? I'm taking away from my children.'" Nevertheless, Annette saw her daily life at home as a little easier now, because her boyfriend spent time with her. As she put it, "It's nice to have help....I don't have to do everything myself." While the "coming home time" was still somewhat difficult, she said, "now it's much easier because I know that if I don't get something done I can do it later. Someone will help me do it later." This change was also reflected in her weekends, which were still spent in family activities but now also included her boyfriend and his help.

Annette depicted herself at this interview as faced with more demands for closeness and relationship than she could handle, and she felt rather helpless to cope with the problem. She expressed positive feelings of relatedness at work and at home but clearly felt somewhat overwhelmed, guilty, and depressed. By the second interview her job orientation had shifted dramatically, and even at home she expressed more of a sense that her home life partly involved "tasks," some of which could be shared or even abandoned.

In short, by the second interview, it was clear that Annette was experiencing less strain in her daily life (this was reflected in her lower stress, anger, and fatigue scores), partly because she had more help at home, and partly because she had lowered her expectations of communality at work.

Michelle: Agentic Orientation to Both Work and Family

In contrast to Annette, Michelle seemed to orient to both her job and her family in an agentic way. At the time of the first interview, Michelle was twenty-three, had been married for about seven years, and had two children under seven. Both before and after the separation, she worked in a factory, on an evening shift, thirty hours a week; she had been doing this job for two and one-half years at the time of the first interview. Her job involved working alone at a highly routinized, somewhat technical task. Michelle characterized her job as "terrible," but said, "It goes by. Some nights seem longer than others."

Since she left for work at three in the afternoon, Michelle's children went directly to a relative's house after school. They played there, had dinner, and were brought home and put to bed. Michelle arrived home long after they had fallen asleep. Perhaps because Michelle and her children lived such different schedules, Michelle described few activities that they did together, indicating that she spent her leisure time alone — reading, watching TV, and baking. Her primary orientation toward her family, then, was administrative or managerial. She organized everyone's time and arranged for everyone's well-being but spent little time in shared activity.

In the first interview Michelle, like Annette, described mornings, especially getting up, as being easier for her since the separation. "[My schedule] is the same; however, I've had all this weight lifted off my shoulders." By contrast, the evenings, coming home at night, were hardest for her, as they were for Annette, but the reason for the difficulty was different: "I guess it was coming home at night....I would walk in the door and the house would just seem so empty. It was always the same, but it was just that feeling of nothingness....it used to hit me like getting hit in the face with a brick or something." She said that she had a hard time falling asleep during this period but would force herself to go to bed at two or three, after a long evening alone. However, she said that this problem did not persist for long, denied that it was serious, and indicated that generally things were going very well.

By the second interview many changes had taken place for this family. Michelle had changed jobs at work and now worked days. She had also moved—she and the children now lived with her fiancé. Michelle was much more positive about her new job; she felt less pressured, which she now reported she had felt before. She spoke more of how she had hated her previous job: "I would get headaches...would feel so drained even before it was time to go in...whereas now it's nothing like that at all."

Michelle indicated that, although she would like to continue working, she wanted to be able to spend more time with her children—even though she was able to spend more time with them than when she worked nights. She spoke of how difficult it had been for her not to see her children very much. But she still did not describe much activity with her children. They went to bed quite early, so there was not much time available in the evening. In the morning, Michelle and her fiancé left for work before the children went to school. Often the children did not eat supper with them. "They eat and they show us their papers....They'll get ready for bed...we talk about school, what they did." Weekends seemed to be the only time the family spent together, and then only when the children weren't visiting their father.

There was, then, by the second year some shift away from the exclusively agentic orientation, but it is not clear how big a shift or how long it will last. A particular problem is understanding Michelle's feelings: while in the first interview she described herself as functioning well (and in fact, her symptom scores were significantly below the sample mean), in the second she told us that in fact she had been quite unhappy and subject to frequent headaches and illness. Bakan suggests that denial and repression are features of unmitigated agency, as the need to master takes precedence over openness. One consequence of this, at least in this case, is that it is difficult to form a clear sense of the person's life and responses from what she says at the time. Perhaps in instances like these retrospective data are actually more useful than data gathered at the time.

Nancy and Elaine: Mixed Orientations

Two women we chose for our case studies described more mixed orientations to work and family. Nancy described an agentic orientation to her job and a communal one toward her family. Nancy was thirty-one at the time of the first interview, had been married ten years before her separation, and had two children, the oldest of whom was nine. She had established a small business just before she got married and she continued working at this business throughout the period of the study. Nancy expressed a great deal of satisfaction with her work and expected to continue in it for the rest of her working life. She hoped to expand her business and was beginning to do so by the second interview.

Nancy worried that she had not devoted much time to her children during her marriage. "I think I didn't give a lot to the kids in all the years we were married because I felt I was supposed to give more to my husband. I think that frustrated me because I didn't have time for them." After the separation, however, she spent much more time with her children. In the beginning she was especially concerned about their reactions to the separation and made a point of being home after school to be with them. One of the things she liked about her job was that she could arrange her schedule around her children. "After school," she said, "we spend [time] together. There've been days we've just stayed home and watched TV. Most of the time we're out—sledding, skating, visiting a friend or maybe just grocery shopping or a few errands....After supper for quite a while we were playing games until bedtime." On weekends it was the same pattern. "Saturday night we're either visiting or spending time together....Either we'll go out for supper or just sit and talk or play a game." Nancy reported in both interviews that she felt good about her life after the separation. She said that now she had about the right amount of time for her work, herself, and her children. "I feel like right now my life is pretty near 90 percent what I want it to be. I'm happy with the kids and I'm putting a lot of my time into them and I'm really enjoying being with them."

Nancy seemed extremely committed to and involved with her business but at the same time delighted by her family relationships. She also expressed more directly than the others a pleasure in being alone. Although she mentioned that at first evenings were hard for her because she would "think over and over in my head what did I do wrong?" she now enjoyed the time alone. "I just love it....I'll just sit there with total silence...and it's like 'oh this feels good.'" While Nancy expressed distress about her divorce (scoring at about the sample mean on the mood scales), she seemed satisfied with her post-separation lifestyle, especially at the second interview, when she seemed less anxious about her children's psychological reactions to the divorce.

Elaine, who expressed a communal orientation to her job but a primarily agentic one toward her family, was in her early thirties, had three children, and had been married a little over ten years when we first saw her. She, like Annette (who reflected a completely communal orientation), worked in a classroom, in group contact with children all day. Elaine's description of her work sounded a great deal like Annette's: "I work in the classroom with the kids....I run around and do crazy things—projects with the kids...read with them...we play a lot of games...take them out on the field." Her work day involved a high level of interpersonal interaction, and she derived satisfaction from the relationships at work. But Elaine's orientation toward her family life was quite different from Annette's. Her children were involved in many extracurricular activities; as she described it, her role in the family was primarily administrative or managerial. She took the children where they needed to go, scheduled and planned their activities, provided meals, and monitored their situations. But she didn't participate with them, nor did she include them in her own outside interests, which included sports, exercise, crafts, and a busy social life.

Elaine, like Annette, sought her divorce and was relieved at the end of her marriage. But, unlike Annette, Elaine found little strain in her new life. She reported that "it's a lot more work because I don't have another person there," that she now had "more responsibilities," and that she used to be able to go out in the evenings more often. But she also said, "I don't mind coming home. I used to hate to come home from work [or] staying home...for any amount of time. So now I don't mind being home....I guess I'm just happier at home now." Elaine reported little significant strain in her daily life, scored at or below the mean on all stress indicators, and said that what she wanted for the future was "to be real independent and do it by myself."

At the time of the follow-up interview, Elaine continued to express little strain. Her classroom work was now only part-time, and she also worked part-time in a medical setting. She continued to derive work satisfactions from relationships with people, but she hoped that her new career would eventually allow her to make more money. She continued to serve as a kind of nodal figure in her children's lives, and in fact encouraged them to take more responsibility for themselves, as she worked two evenings a week. Thus, the eldest child (who was then twelve) prepared dinner for the others once or twice a week, and all the children were urged to settle conflicts and problems among themselves—although she was available to serve as a telephone referee when they could not. At this point Elaine reported very little stress in her daily life; in fact, she was unable to identify a difficult part of her day.

Overview

The four cases seem to illustrate some valuable points. First, unmitigated communion, or too much relationship without any opportunity for independent action, seemed to undermine the individual's sense of competence and to result in a sense of helplessness and negative feelings. Unmitigated agency, or not enough connectedness, was also stressful but was expressed at the time only in a sense of emptiness, or a lack. It was only retrospectively that the period of lack of connectedness was understood to have been one of real unhappiness and physical illness.

Interestingly, the women who expressed solely agentic and solely communal orientations at the first interview experienced the greatest change in their life situations. Both of them had found a new partner to bring into the household, thus transforming their families somewhat, and their work activities and aspirations had also shifted. By the second interview both women expressed orientations involving more of a mixture of agentic and communal concerns. The two women who originally had more mixed orientations, on the other hand, expressed less strain in the first interview and had made fewer changes in their lives by the second.

We can generalize little from these four case studies of divorcing mothers, but we were struck by how well the women's reports of their experiences fit the hypotheses derived from our extension of Bakan's notion. It seemed plausible that unmitigated communion, not families, promotes depression; that unmitigated agency, not jobs, promotes denial and illness; and that the balancing of agency and communion, not combining jobs and families, allows women to manage stress and change, even of a drastic sort, with an amazing grace. Given the confirmation of our conceptualization in the case studies, we developed a method for coding all of the interviews so we could explore our hypothesis in more quantitative and generalizable terms.

Content Analysis of Interviews

Coding Agency and Communion

In order to pursue more systematically the notion of agency and communion, we developed a method by which to code the interviews with all of the 102 recently separated women in the sample for agency and communion in the workplace and at home. (See table 4.2 for examples of coding categories.) Using Bakan's definitions as a source, we coded as agentic any expressions reflecting individual initiative, separate tasks or activities, or independent spheres of action. *Individual initiative* is expressed in taking on specific tasks or general responsibilities (for example, arranging your own work schedule or managing your children's activities). *Separate tasks or activities* involve working independently on a task or doing things alone (typing or filing at work, reading at home). *Independent spheres of action* concern responsibility for a general area of activity (managing the payroll or seeing that all the housework gets done). *Collective actions* involve working together on tasks or doing things together (sharing job responsibilities at work, or working together on housework, homework, leisure activities). *Mutual dependence* reflects providing support to and receiving support from another (working as a team at the office or experiencing mutual support from a friend). *Relationships* are assessed in terms of expression of interest in maintaining or enhancing friendships or family relationships (becoming good friends with someone or wanting to be closer to the children).

Coding was based on open-ended responses to a series of interview questions about each woman's (and her children's) daily routine at home (including her leisure activities) and at work. (Questions included: "Describe a typical day during the week"; "How do you spend your time when you are not with the children?"; "What are your major tasks or responsibilities at work?") All responses reflecting communion or agency, accord-

Table 4.2: *Coding Categories for
Agency and Communion in Work and Family Life*

Category	Examples
Agency	
Individual initiative	"I do my own procedures . . . schedule my own patients."
	"I supervise their homework and organize their after-school activities."
Separate tasks and activities	"I do the secretarial things—typing, filing, things like that."
	"They play games and do their homework; I read and listen to my music."
Independent spheres of action	"I handle the leases and rents."
	"I get supper ready and do the chores around the house."
Communion	
Collective action	"We try to work out the overall strategies together—often over lunch."
	"I read to the kids before bed; we all lie on the bed together and we all read."
Mutual dependence	"We make a good team—together we're an unbeatable combination."
	"We all work together to get dinner on the table—Betsy sets the table, and Maureen makes the salad, while I cook."
Relationships	"We get along very well—in fact we're really close and can count on each other."
	"We talk about how their day has gone. I like being with the kids and enjoying them, and having a good time. We're real close."

ing to the coding categories, either in subjects' descriptions of their current situation or their expressed wishes for increased agency or communion, were coded. Detailed information about home life was obtained in both interviews; however, only at the second interview were specific questions concerning employment asked. Because more complete employment data was obtained at the second interview, we limited our analyses to information obtained at that time. Once the codebook was finalized, expert coding was established for a random subset of the interviews. A graduate student, blind to the hypotheses of the study, was trained in the coding system, obtaining reliability with the expert coding of .90; she subsequently coded all the interviews. Since we hoped to derive an overall score for relative degrees of agentic and communal experience in work and family life, we coded each mention of an agentic or communal orientation. A total score for agency and communion was obtained by adding the number of occurrences of each orientation across all areas of home, work, and relationships.

Women's emotional and physical health was defined in terms of three scores based on factor analyses of a variety of indicators. The three factors were identical in analyses of data taken at both interviews and were therefore considered stable. The scale measuring *emotional health* was composed of four of the subscales of the Profile of Mood States (POMS; McNair, Lorr, and Droppleman, 1971). Many studies have demonstrated that the POMS significantly differentiates a variety of emotionally distraught clinical samples from samples of adults not experiencing emotional distress, and that it is sensitive to efforts either to arouse or to ameliorate emotional disturbance (see McNair, Lorr, and Droppleman, 1971, for a review of validity studies). Moreover, McNair and his colleagues present impressive evidence for the internal consistency and test-retest reliability of the scales comprising the total mood disturbance score. For our purposes, the scales measuring anger-hostility, confusion-bewilderment, depression-dejection, and tension-anxiety were reverse-scored and combined to create an overall indicator of emotional health.

A general *well-being* score was created by standard-scoring and summing the Rosenberg (1965) self-esteem scale, a measure of life satisfaction, and the vigor-activity scale from the POMS. The Rosenberg scale was originally designed as a unidimensional tool for assessing self-esteem in a brief format; thus, the scale includes only ten items. Silber and Tippett (1965) report test-retest correlations of .85 over a two-week period and substantial correlations with other measures of similar constructs. Moreover, Rosenberg (1965) presents supporting evidence of the construct validity of the scale, citing positive correlations with many social and interpersonal variables (for example, less shyness and depression, more assertiveness). In addition to self-esteem, the vigor-activity scale and a single life-satisfaction item similar to that used by Gurin, Veroff, and Feld (1960) and Bradburn and Caplovitz (1965) contributed to the overall well-being score.

Finally, each mother completed a questionnaire on physical symptoms adapted from the national studies of Gurin, Veroff, and Feld (1960) and Veroff, Kulka, and Douvan (1981). This measure has been well-established as a reliable and valid indicator of psychological symptoms in these nationwide studies of mental health in adults. Scores from this measure and a health questionnaire assessing common illnesses (colds, headaches, and so on), based on those developed by others (see Wahler, 1973; Abramson et al., 1965), were standardized, reverse-scored, and combined to create an overall measure of *physical health*.

Results of Content Analyses

The women's total agency and communion scores were divided at the

Table 4.3: *Agency and Communion Concerns and Mental and Physical Health among Divorcing Mothers*

Emotional health					
		Communion score			
		low	high		
	low	52.05[a]	46.35[a,b]	Fagency	= 86
Agency score		(40)	(29)	Fcommunion	= .13
	high	48.65	53.06[b]	Finteraction	= 8.06**
		(17)	(16)		
Well-being					
		Communion score			
		low	high		
	low	50.20	48.55[b]	Fagency	= 1.29
Agency score		(40)	(29)	Fcommunion	= 1.68
	high	48.29[a]	54.13[a,b]	Finteraction	= 5.38*
		(17)	(16)		
Physical health					
		Communion score			
		low	high		
	low	49.38	51.10	Fagency	= .17
Agency score		(40)	(29)	Fcommunion	= 5.45*
	high	47.53[a]	54.50[a]	Finteraction	= 1.98
		(17)	(16)		

Note: Numbers in parentheses are the *N*s for that cell. Unequal *N*s resulted from the relatively low agency scores for the sample as a whole. Means with a common superscript are significantly different from each other in the post-hoc analyses.
*p < .05   **p < .01

median; two-way analyses of variance were performed on physical health, emotional health, and well-being (table 4.3).

Women either high or low on both agency and communion scored significantly higher on emotional health than women high in communion and low in agency. For well-being, only women high in both agency and communion scored significantly higher than women high in only one. Finally, for physical health, there was a main effect for communion (women were higher in physical health if they were high in communion). Interestingly, though, this effect was strongest for those women high in agency. Thus, the benefits of high communion were greatest for those women high in agency. Balanced agency and communion, regardless of level, predicted emotional health, balanced high agency and communion predicted well-being, and communion among those high in agency predicted physical health. Thus balance predicted internal experience, and mitigated agency predicted better physical health.

In order to evaluate the effects of agency and communion on depression, we performed a two-way analysis of variance on the depression-dejection scale of the POMS (table 4.4). Balanced agency and communion, regardless of level, was associated with lower levels of depression. Thus, depression did not seem exclusively associated with unmitigated communion.

Table 4.4: *Agency and Communion Concerns and Depression in Divorcing Mothers*

		Communion score			
		low	high		
	low	7.63	13.76	Fagency	= .48
Agency score		(40)	(29)	Fcommunion	= .01
	high	12.29	6.44	Finteraction	= 9.72**
		(17)	(16)		

Note: Numbers in parentheses are the Ns for those cells.
**$p < .01$

We carried out a final series of analyses using the women's work status as a predictor of the emotional and physical health variables, in order to determine whether role combination per se predicted mental and physical health (table 4.5). There were no significant differences among divorcing mothers who did not work outside the home, who worked part-time, or who worked full-time. There was a trend for the full-time working mothers to score higher on the physical health scale than the other two groups.

Interestingly, although role combination itself was not a strong predictor of emotional and physical health, it was related to the agency-communion

Table 4.5: *Work Status and Mental and Physical Health*
in Divorcing Mothers

Emotional health		
No employment outside the home	48.33	
Part-time employment	50.15	F = .42
Full-time employment	50.48	
Well-being		
No employment outside the home	50.28	
Part-time employment	50.04	F = .01
Full-time employment	49.95	
Physical health		
No employment outside the home	48.06	
Part-time employment	48.08	F = 2.66**
Full-time employment	52.10	

Note: 18 women were not employed outside the home; 26 were employed
part-time; and 58 full-time.
**$p < .01$

pattern ($\chi^2 = 20.66$, $p < .01$; see table 4.6). Women with no employment
outside the home were especially likely to be low in agency and high in
communion (56% of those women compared with 15% of part-time workers and 26% of full-time workers). Part-time workers, in contrast, were
particularly likely to be low in both agency and communion (69% of them,
compared with 11% of nonemployed women and 35% of full-time employed women). Full-time employed women were somewhat more likely
to be high in agency and low in communion (22% of them, compared with
11% of nonemployed women and 8% of part-time workers). It should be

Table 4.6: *Relationship between Work Status and Pattern of Agency*
and Communion Concerns

	Number of women		
	No employment	*Part-time employment*	*Full-time employment*
Low agency, low communion	2	18	20
Low agency, high communion	10	4	15
High agency, low communion	2	2	13
High agency, high communion	4	2	10

noted, though, that full-time employed women were found in substantial numbers with all four patterns (17% high-high; 22% high agency, low communion; 26% low agency, high communion, 35% low-low). Thus, role combination was related to agency-communion pattern to some degree, but it was the agency-communion pattern that predicted emotional and physical health.

Both the case study and the systematic content analysis supported the notion that the balanced presence of agency and communion facilitates emotional and physical health, at least for this sample of (presumably stressed) divorcing mothers of school-age children. There is, moreover, evidence that role combination per se does *not* predict physical or emotional health, though it is moderately predictive of the pattern of agency and communion concerns as expressed in the women's interview responses.

Results of both the case studies and the systematic content analysis failed to support any special relationship between unmitigated communion and depression, though unmitigated communion was associated with lower health and well-being more generally. Thus, for example, Michelle reported fatigue, anger, and stress symptoms—not simply depression. Moreover, depression seemed to result from an imbalance of *either* agency or communion and seemed to be prevented by balanced presence *or* absence of both. It is possible that unmitigated agency and unmitigated communion result in different types of depression, but for the present we can only conclude that unmitigated communion is unhealthy, not specifically that it is depressing.

There is, however, support for the notion (first proposed by Bakan) that unmitigated agency has consequences for physical health. First, the case study of Annette suggested that the unmitigated agency was experienced as stressful and associated with physical symptoms (in this case, headaches). Moreover, in the quantitative analysis, the benefits of communion for physical health were marked (statistically significant) only for those women high in agency. Thus, women high in agency and low in communion were at the greatest risk of physical illness in this sample.

These results suggest that an important focus for future research on life stress and role combination should be the pattern of agency and communion concerns reflected in women's (and perhaps men's) lives. Apparently these human needs and gifts can and must be expressed, regardless of the pattern of roles and relationships in our life structure, if we are to lead satisfying and healthy lives.

References

Abramson, J. H., Terespolsky, L., Brook, J. G., and Clark, S. L. (1965). Cornell Medical Index as a health measure in epidemiological studies: A test of the validity of a health questionnaire. *British Journal of Preventive Medicine*, 19, 102–10.

Bakan, D. (1966). *The duality of human existence*. Boston: Beacon Press.

Baruch, G. K., Barnett, R. C., and Rivers, C. (1984). *Lifeprints: New patterns of love and work for today's women*. New York: New American Library.

Belle, D. (ed.) (1982). *Lives in stress: Women and depression*. Beverly Hills: Sage.

Bradburn, N., and Caplovitz, D. (1965). *Reports on happiness*. Chicago: Aldine.

Gurin, G., Veroff, J., and Feld, S. (1960). *Americans view their mental health*. New York: Basic Books.

Ibrahim, M. A. (1980). The changing health state of women. *American Journal of Public Health*, 70, 120–21.

McNair, D., Lorr, M., and Droppleman, L. (1971). *Profile of mood states*. San Diego: Educational and Industrial Testing Service.

Rosenberg, M. (1965). *Society and the adolescent self-image*. Princeton: Princeton University Press.

Silber, E., and Tippett, J. (1965). Self-esteem: Clinical assessment and measurement validation. *Psychological Reports*, 16, 1017–71.

Stewart, A. J., and Salt, P. (1981). Life stress, life-styles, depression and illness in adult women. *Journal of Personality and Social Psychology*, 40 (6), 1063–69.

Verbrugge, L. M. (1982). Women's social roles and health. In P. Berman and E. Ramey (eds.), *Women: A developmental perspective*. Bethesda, Md.: National Institute of Mental Health, Publication no. 82–2298.

Veroff, J., Kulka, R. A., and Douvan, E. (1981). *Mental health in America*. New York: Basic Books.

Wahler, H. J. (1973). *Wahler physical symptoms inventory*. Western Psychological Services.

5

Role Quality and Psychological Well-Being

Grace K. Baruch and Rosalind C. Barnett

What is the relationship between involvement in multiple roles and well-being in midlife women? Sociologists and psychologists have long been interested in how women who occupy different roles differ in well-being. Two major hypotheses have been put forward concerning the relation of role involvement and well-being among women. The *scarcity hypothesis* assumes that the social structure normally creates overly demanding role obligations (Goode, 1960). The more roles one occupies, the more obligations one faces. Because human energy is limited, well-being is impaired by overload and by conflict between incompatible roles. The *expansion hypothesis*, on the other hand, emphasizes the benefits rather than the costs of multiple involvement (Marks, 1977; Sieber, 1974). Benefits include status, privileges, increased self-esteem, and the ability to trade off undesirable components of roles. Like placing one's eggs in many baskets, involvement in several roles, according to this view, is likely to mean having a variety of sources of stimulation, gratification, and social validation.

Both the expansion and the scarcity hypotheses are limited by their focus on the number of roles occupied; both fail to examine how particular roles or the quality of experience within a role might contribute to or impair well-being. The expansion hypothesis, for example, assumes a net gain of benefits over costs regardless of the nature of the roles a person occupies. Our view, in contrast, is that what most affects well-being is not the

The research reported here was supported by NSF No. BNS 77–26756 and conducted while the authors were at Brandeis University. The authors extend their appreciation to Erin Phelps and Nancy Marshall for their assistance in data analysis and to Nathalie Dana Thompson for her assistance in manuscript preparation.

63

number of roles but rather the specific roles occupied and their quality. The experience of a woman who occupies the two roles of wife and mother, for example, may differ from that of a woman who occupies the roles of wife and paid worker. The psychological consequences of occupying multiple roles, furthermore, depends not only on the number of roles a woman plays but also on how much she enjoys each role.

In this chapter we look at the associations between role occupancy and psychological functioning among a sample of 238 women interviewed in 1979 and 1980 (Baruch, Barnett, and Rivers, 1985). The sample was drawn in such a way as to include various family role patterns while also taking into account employment status. As table 5.1 shows, the study included women in four family patterns: never married, married without children, married with children, and divorced with children. Half of the married women and all the never-married and divorced women were employed outside the home. Employed women within each family pattern were drawn equally from high, medium, and low prestige occupations (Siegel, 1971). Nonemployed women were stratified similarly by the prestige level of their husbands' occupations.

Table 5.1: *Role Patterns Selected for the Study*

| | Family Roles | | | |
| | Never married | Married without children | Married with children | Divorced with children |
Work Roles				
Employed	n = 49	n = 40	n = 46	n = 46
Not employed	—	n = 15	n = 42	—

Note: It was not possible to locate the desired number of married, childless, non-employed women. Economic pressures and ideological changes have apparently made this role pattern very rare. There were 238 women in the sample.

Like previous researchers, we analyze well-being as a function of the number of roles a woman occupies, but unlike most previous researchers we concentrate on the *quality* of the women's experiences in the various roles. For the three life roles that we examine—worker, wife, and mother—we document the nature of the rewards and costs and measure the extent to which the rewards of each role outweigh its costs. By creating a numeric score—which we call a Balance Score—for each woman in the sample that reflects the balance of rewards and costs in each of her life roles, we can determine which matters more for psychological well-being: role occupancy or role quality.

The Survey of Women in Midlife

To examine the relationships between role occupancy, role quality, and well-being, we conducted a two-stage interview study of women aged thirty-five to fifty-five living in a Massachusetts community. The community was selected because of its heterogeneous population. By the end of the study, we had telephoned over six thousand women in the community to locate enough women for each of the sampling categories. The names were drawn randomly from voting lists.

The first stage of the study consisted of intensive, semi-structured interviews lasting three to six hours with a "snowball" or convenience sample of twelve women from each of the six categories. The women varied not only in employment and family role status but in the number of major social roles—wife, mother, paid worker—they occupied. A major goal of these interviews was to identify the rewarding and distressing aspects of roles so that a survey instrument could be designed.

In the second stage of the study, we aimed to select randomly approximately forty-five women in each of six role patterns. The women classified as employed had all been working at least seventeen hours a week for at least three months prior to being interviewed. In order to ensure that subjects were not in an acute state of crisis, women whom we chose for the divorced category had been divorced or legally separated for at least one year prior to the interview. Interestingly, we were able to fill all the categories save one. We could locate only fifteen women who were married, childless, and not in the paid labor market. The rarity of the category seems informative in itself. The mean age of the entire sample was 43.6 years and the mean total family income was $21,600. Overall, the sample had an average of fourteen years of education—two years beyond high school. All of the women in the study were Caucasian. Of the mothers, thirty had children under eight and eighty-nine had children aged eight to eighteen living at home.

Survey Instrument

Our focus was on the quality of a woman's experiences in her social roles and on how the quality of life roles relates to psychological well-being. The first task, therefore, was to construct a numeric measure of the quality of each role. During the in-depth interviews in the first stage of the study, we asked the women to describe and assess their various life experiences. Their descriptions allowed us to construct lists of frequently mentioned rewards and concerns in each of the three roles.

For the paid worker role, the lists contained nineteen positive items—such as "hours fit your needs" and "variety of tasks"—and nineteen negative items—such as "having too much to do" and "job insecurity." The fifteen rewards of the wife role included such items as "companionship" and "having someone to take care of you"; and the fifteen concerns included items such as "husband being unavailable" and "poor communication." For the mother role, we constructed a list with fourteen rewards, such as "being needed" and "pleasure from children's accomplishments," and fourteen concerns, such as "financial strain" and "feeling trapped and bored."

Each participant in the second stage of the study used a four-point scale to indicate for every relevant role the extent to which each item proved rewarding or distressing. For each participant in each role we calculated three numeric scores: a reward score (her average response to the reward items), a concern score (her average response to the concern items), and a balance score (rewards minus concerns). The balance score constituted our major index of the quality of experience within a role.

We employed three indices of psychological well-being. The first was a standard measure of self-esteem, the Rosenberg Self-Esteem Scale (Rosenberg, 1965). Items included five positive statements such as "I feel I have a number of good qualities" and five negative statements such as "I certainly feel useless at times." For each statement, respondents indicated their responses on a four-point scale from "strongly agree" to "strongly disagree." The depression subscale of the Hopkins Symptom Checklist constituted the second measure of well-being (Derogatis et al., 1974). On this scale, including eleven items, respondents indicated on a five-point scale from "not at all" to "extremely" how frequently during the previous week they felt lonely, fearful, hopeless, or blue. The final measure of well-being we called a Pleasure Scale. It contained three standard single-item measures of happiness, satisfaction, and optimism. Respondents were asked, for example, "Taking all things together, how would you say things are these days...would you say you're *very* happy, *pretty* happy, or *not too* happy these days?" The Pleasure Scale was internally reliable, with an alpha coefficient of .76.

Role Quality: Balance of Rewards and Concerns

Which items, from our lists of rewards and concerns for each role, were rated as most rewarding or distressing by the women interviewed during the second stage of the study? Table 5.2 presents the top-ranking

Table 5.2: Ranking of the Rewards and Concerns of Life Roles

Roles	Rewards	Concerns	No. of Women	No. of Items
Paid Worker	Being able to work on one's own (3.57)	Having too much to do (2.16)		19 pos. 19 neg.
	Sense of accomplishment (3.47)	Having to juggle conflicting tasks (2.04)	n = 180	
	Having a job that fits one's interest and skills (3.23)	Lacking career growth opportunities (1.95)		
Wife	Companionship (3.48)	Husband's physical health problems (2.08)		15 pos. 15 neg.
	Having a husband who backs one up in what one wants to do (3.45)	Conflicts over the children (1.89)	n = 142	
	Having a husband who sees one as special (3.44)	Husband's job problems (1.70)		
Mother	The love the children show (3.72)	Worry about children's physical well-being (2.37)		14 pos. 14 neg.
	Liking the kind of people the children are (3.67)	Worry about teenage years (2.36)	n = 136	
	Pleasure from children's accomplishments (3.63)	Financial stress (2.20)		

The numbers in parentheses are the average rankings of each item on a 1–4 scale. The higher the number, the more positive the reward or the more distressing the concern.

rewards and concerns for the roles of paid worker, wife, and mother. The table displays the average score, from 1 to 4, that each received. For example, the reward item "being able to work on one's own" received an average evaluation of 3.57 from the 180 employed women in the sample.

It is human nature to focus on the positive aspects of life and to underplay the negative, and the women in our sample proved no exception. As can be seen in table 5.2, the women in our study reported higher levels of rewards than of concerns, resulting in positive balance scores for each role, calculated by subtracting the average concern score from the average reward score of each woman in that role. In theory the overall average balance score for each role could range from +3 to -3. If all 180 of the paid workers in the survey, for example, gave each of the nineteen positive items on our list of job rewards the highest possible score (4) and each item on our list of nineteen job concerns the lowest possible score (1), the net result would be a score of +3. Conversely, if all the employees gave each concern the highest possible score and each reward the lowest, the net result would be -3. The actual average balance scores were 1.35 for the role of paid worker, 1.67 for the wife role, and 1.47 for the mother role. For each role, the respondents tended to rate the rewards as greater than the concerns.

Not only did the women feel more positively than negatively about their life roles, but the results suggest that the more roles a woman occupied the happier she tended to feel with each particular role. Table 5.3 presents the balance scores for each role relevant to each category of women. Unmarried working women had the lowest balance score for the role of paid worker. Conversely, the balance scores for the wife role were greatest among women who occupied all three roles. This pattern is in accord with studies conducted by Crosby (1982, 1984; Bersoff and Crosby, 1984) in which paid

Table 5.3: *Mean Balance Scores of the Role Pattern Groups*

		Role		
		Paid worker	*Wife*	*Mother*
Group	Paid worker	1.16	—	—
	Wife	—	1.69	—
	Wife, mother	—	1.58	1.57
	Paid worker, wife	1.53	1.61	—
	Paid worker, mother	1.29	—	1.33
	Paid worker, wife, mother	1.46	1.80	1.52
	Overall	1.35	1.67	1.47

Note: The balance score represents the average value assigned to the rewards of the roles minus the average value assigned to the costs. The scores could range, theoretically, from −3 to +3.

employment was shown to enhance satisfaction with domestic life among women and parenthood to enhance satisfaction with work among women and men.

Role Occupancy, Role Quality, and Well-Being

How do roles women play and their experiences in these roles affect their psychological well-being? Given that people tend to experience the rewards of role occupancy as greater than the costs, do variations in role quality predict variation in well-being beyond what is accounted for by role occupancy? To answer these questions, we examine our data in several ways.

Our first approach to the data is descriptive. We can simply look at variations in well-being among the women in different role patterns. Table 5.4 shows the self-esteem, depression, and pleasure scores of the various role pattern groups. Both self-esteem and depression scores remained virtually constant across all groups in the study. Pleasure, the score composed of three items tapping happiness, satisfaction, and optimism, was much higher among some groups of women than among others. Interestingly, pleasure was greatest among the employed married women (and especially among the employed married mothers).

Table 5.4: *Well-being among Women in Varying Role Patterns*

	Never married		Married, childless		Married, mothers		Divorced mothers	
Employed	SE =	3.37	SE =	3.57	SE =	3.59	SE =	3.56
	D =	1.48	D =	1.38	D =	1.33	D =	1.38
	P =	−0.94	P =	0.28	P =	0.72	P =	0.05
Not employed			SE =	3.35	SE =	3.30		
			D =	1.48	D =	1.35		
			P =	−0.69	P =	−0.45		

Note: SE = mean self-esteem score; theoretical range 1–4; the higher the score, the more positive.

D = depression score; theoretical range 1–4; the higher the score, the more depressed.

P = mean pleasure score. This is a standardized score: +1.00 indicates one standard deviation above the overall mean, and −1.00 indicates one standard deviation below.

A second way to look at the associations between role occupancy or role quality and the indices of psychological well-being is to examine the inter-correlations among measures. Intercorrelations allow us to address various questions. Most basically, do the three different measures of well-being vary together? That is, does a woman's self-esteem tell us anything about her feelings of depression or of pleasure? Second, and more important, does the number of roles a woman occupies predict self-esteem, depression, and pleasure scores? Finally, and most important, what are the associations between role quality (as indexed by a balance score) and the three aspects of psychological functioning?

Table 5.5, which presents the correlations, provides some answers. First, it is clear that the three indicators of well-being were moderately related to each other, as one would expect. Second, the number of roles a woman occupied was indicative of well-being, but only mildly. Much more important than the number of roles was the quality of a woman's experiences in her roles. How positive a woman felt about her marriage, for example, was very strongly related to how much pleasure she took in life generally. The two measures correlated at .70.

Table 5.5: *Correlations among Measures (for the entire sample)*

	Psychological Well-being		
	Self-esteem	*Depression*	*Pleasure*
Depression	− .63***	—	—
Pleasure	.51***	− .61**	—
Number of roles	.16**	− .14*	.23***
Quality of worker role	.36**	− .35***	.49***
Quality of wife role	.35***	− .45***	.70***
Quality of mother role	.34***	.42***	.34***

* p < .05   ** p < .01   *** p < .001

The relationships between role quality and well-being are very strong. But what does this mean? The apparent relationships could be artifacts of a woman's age, educational level, or family income, since the groups of women with various role patterns also differed somewhat on these characteristics. Overall, employment status correlated significantly with education among our sample $(r = .25; p < .001)$, and marital status correlated significantly with income $(r = .26; p < .001)$. Perhaps the women who expressed positive feelings about their roles as paid worker or as wife, for example, differed from other women in terms of education or income, and perhaps these related, but masked, variations were actually responsible for the differences in well-being.

Our final task, therefore, was to determine how much of the variations in well-being were due to the quality of women's experiences in various roles *after* one took into account the demographic characteristics and the number of roles occupied. Hierarchical multiple regression analysis is a statistical procedure whereby we can look at the relationships between variables of interest while holding constant additional variables (such as age or education). We conducted three such analyses. In the first, we determined the extent to which variations in the women's self-esteem scores were due to variations in the quality of their roles, over and above the effects of (1) education, age, and family income and (2) the number of roles they occupied. We then repeated the procedures for depression and pleasure (table 5.6).

Table 5.6 confirms the soundness of the relationship between the quality of women's role experiences and their psychological well-being. It indi-

Table 5.6: *Hierarchical Multiple Regression Analyses of Well-being Indices*

Predictors	Step	Self-esteem $B^†$	Depression $B^†$	Pleasure
Control Variables	1			
Education		.04	.07	.11
Age		−.04	−.08	.02
Family income		.25***	.24***	.34***
R² for step 1		.07	.06	.11
Role Occupancy Variables	2			
Paid worker		.20**	−.03	.05
Wife		−.05	−.07	−.01
Mother		.06	−.10	.13
R² for step 2		.11	.07	.13
Quality of Experience Variables	3‡			
Paid worker		.20**	−.23***	.31***
Wife		.16*	−.23***	.47***
Mother		.18**	−.19**	.09
R² for step 3		.22**	.23**	.46***

†Standardized regression coefficient for variable entered into regression at that step
‡Delta R² calculations indicated that this step produced a significant increment in variance explained.
*p < .05   **p < .01   ***p < .001.

cates, first, that family income statistically predicts all three measures of well-being. The wealthier a woman was, the higher was her self-esteem, the greater was her pleasure, and the lower her feelings of depression. Second, the mere occupancy of life roles did not, by and large, enhance well-being. Paid workers tended to have higher self-esteem than other women in our sample, but employment status did not relate to depression or pleasure, nor did depression or pleasure depend on a woman's status as a mother or a wife. The lack of association between marital status and pleasure, evident in table 5.6, contrasts with the distributions in table 5.4 and allows us to infer that the enhanced sense of pleasure evident in married employed women (and especially married employed mothers) resulted not only from the pattern of their roles but also from something about the age or level of education and income among those groups.

The final message of table 5.6 is that women's well-being, almost without exception, corresponded closely to the quality of their roles. The greater the gap between the rewards and costs of the worker role, the higher was a woman's self-esteem and the greater were her freedom from depression and her sense of pleasure in life. The same pattern emerged concerning the role of wife. The quality of the mothering role did not relate to a woman's sense of pleasure in life, but it did predict both self-esteem and depression scores.

The findings of our survey of women in midlife carry implications for the debate between the theorists who emphasize role stress and those who focus on the benefits of role accumulation. It seems to us no longer useful to argue over the question of how many roles a woman ought to occupy, because role occupancy per se predicts little about well-being. What really matters is the nature of the experiences within a role. Those concerned with women's mental health should now, therefore, turn their attention to understanding how to enhance the quality of women's experiences within each of their many roles.

References

Baruch, G. K., Barnett, R. C., and Rivers, C. (1985). *Lifeprints: New patterns of love and work for today's women*. New York: Signet.

Bersoff, D., and Crosby, F. (1984). Job satisfaction and family status. *Personality and Social Psychology Bulletin*, 10, 75–83.

Crosby, F. (1982). *Relative deprivation and working women*. New York: Oxford University Press.

————. (1984). Job satisfaction and domestic life. In M. D. Lee and R. N. Kunango (eds.), *Management of work and personal life*. New York: Praeger, 41–60.

Delongis, A., Coyne, J. C., Dakof, G., Folkman, S., and Lazarus, R. S. (1982). Relationship of daily hassles, uplifts, and major life events to health status. *Health Psychology*, 1, 119–36.

Derogatis, L. R., Lipman, R. S., Rickels, K., Uhlenhuth, E. H., and Coti, L. (1974). The Hopkins Symptom Checklist. In P. Pichot (ed.), *Psychological measurements in psychopharmacology*. Paris: Karger, Basel.

Goode, W. J. (1960). A theory of strain. *American Sociological Review*, 25, 483–96.

Marks, S. R. (1977). Multiple roles and role strain: Some notes on human energy, time and commitment. *American Sociological Review*, 41, 921–36.

Rosenberg, M. (1965). *Society and the adolescent self-image*. Princeton: Princeton University Press.

Sieber, S. D. (1974). Toward a theory of role accumulation. *American Sociological Review*, 39, 567–78.

Siegel, P. M. (1971). Prestige in the American occupational structure. Ph. D. diss., University of Chicago.

6

Marital Influence Levels and Symptomatology among Wives

Janice M. Steil and Beth A. Turetsky

Jessie Bernard (1973) was among the first to proclaim that marriage is not as good for women as it is for men. According to her, a review of epidemiological data shows that married women are more likely than married men to become depressed and otherwise psychologically impaired. Despite subsequent methodological controversy and empirical debate (Bachrach, 1975; Dohrenwend and Dohrenwend, 1976; Gove and Tudor, 1977), there is strong support for Bernard's assertion (Gove, 1972; Gove and Tudor, 1973; Radloff, 1975). Yet why such differences should exist is unclear. Several ideas have been posed but none has proved fully explanatory (Clancey and Gove, 1974; Gove, 1972; Gove and Tudor, 1973; Phillips and Segal, 1969; Weissman and Klerman, 1977).

Recent reviews have proposed that the differences in husbands' and wives' psychological well-being may be explained by differences in marital power (Steil, 1983, 1984). Research consistently shows that wives have less influence in their marital relationships than their husbands do (Beckman and Houser, 1979; Gilbert, 1985; Mason and Bumpass, 1975; Weingarten, 1978; Steil, 1983). According to the social exchange theorists, wives lack influence because relative to their husbands they provide few outside resources to the family (Homans, 1961; Scanzoni, 1972; Thibaut and Kelley, 1959). Indeed, numerous investigators have linked people's influence within their marriages to their employment outside of the family. Employed wives have been found to have more say at home than housewives (Beckman and Houser, 1979; Crosby, 1982; Mason and Bumpass, 1978). Similarly, the greater a husband's occupational prestige, the more he dom-

74

inates domestic decisions (Ericksen, Yancey, and Ericksen, 1979). In short, gender differences in marital influence parallel gender differences in occupational resources outside marriage.

The link between marital power and psychological well-being has been suggested by evidence of parallels between them. It has been shown, for example, that housewives experience the least influence within their marriages and the highest levels of distress, while employed husbands have the most influence and experience the least distress. Employed wives fall somewhere in between on both measures (Gove and Geerken, 1977; Radloff, 1975). Indeed, the patterns are strong enough that a presidential subpanel on mental health and women (1978) asserted that "our usual social institutions (including, among others, marriage, family relations, and child rearing) have a differential and more stressful impact on women" (Report of Special Populations Subpanel, 1978:1). Yet circumstantial evidence can carry us only so far. The study reported in this chapter goes beyond previous work by providing a more direct test of the link between marital power and psychological well-being suggested in earlier work.

In addition, this study looks beyond the mere fact of female employment. Instead of dividing our sample of women into employees and housewives, we investigate how the occupational resources of a group of employed professional women relate to their marital influence and ask whether there exists among professional women the association between earning power and domestic power that researchers have so often found among men. To examine the links, we use data collected from professionally employed, married women. We have information on each woman's economic resources outside the marriage, her influence and responsibilities within the marriage, and her psychological well-being. We use the information to help determine whether a woman with more resources outside marriage will have more influence within marriage, and whether this is related to psychological functioning. We are interested as well in learning more about how the presence of children affects marital influence. That children change the marital dynamics is well established. Exactly how they affect the expected links between occupational resources, marital responsibilities, and well-being remains unclear. Are resource variables a better predictor of marital influence for mothers than for childless women? Is marital equality associated more closely with psychological well-being among mothers than among women without children?

The Study

The Sample

Study participants were 815 dual-career couples who were questioned in 1980 by Catalyst. Of the participants, 40 percent lived in the Northeast and the rest came from all over the United States. Career was defined as attitudinal on the part of the individual, encompassing expectations of life-long work characterized by strong commitment, personal growth, and increasing levels of responsibility. In all instances the wife had a career in the business community. Approximately 15% had job titles of vice president or director, 3% had the title assistant vice president, almost 17% were managers, 33% had the title professional staff, 5% were administrators, and the remaining 26.5% were categorized at lower levels. Forty-four percent of the women were college graduates. Another 33% had postgraduate degrees. More than 60% of the wives were between the ages of 26 and 35. Median number of years in the career was five and the mean income of the woman was $23,451. Forty percent of the couples had children. Respondents were solicited by Catalyst, a national nonprofit organization that works to foster the full participation of women in corporate and professional life. Announcements were placed by Catalyst in selected magazines and in a nationally syndicated United Press International column.

Instruments

Husbands and wives independently completed identical six-page questionnaires aimed at assessing the stresses particular to the dual-career couple. Areas of inquiry included educational and employment demographics, factors affecting location and relocation decisions, advantages and disadvantages of combining career and family, family and career satisfaction, allocation of domestic and decision-making responsibilities, mental health symptomatology, and achievement concerns. Our study utilized specific subsets of the data to examine the variables shown in table 6.1.

Resources. Within the marital context, resources have been defined as "anything that one partner may make available to the other, helping the latter satisfy his (her) needs or attain his (her) goals" (Blood and Wolfe, 1960:12). Typically, researchers believe that economic resources, as compared to nurturant resources, play a disproportionate role in determining marital influence (Kidder, Fagan, and Cohen, 1980; Steil, 1983, 1984). Two demographic, two economic, and one psychological resource variable were assessed. The wife's age and educational level were subtracted from her husband's to form the age and education discrepancy variables. The wife's absolute income was assessed and used as a variable and the wife's income was also subtracted from her husband's to form the pay discrepancy variable. Finally, a 3-point scale was used to assess the wife's perception of the importance of her own career as compared to her husband's (1 = wife's more important; 2 = both equally important; 3 = husband's more important).

Tables 6.1: *Variables Assessed in the Study*

Resources	Marital Influence and Responsibility	Well-being
Wife's earnings	Equality of decision-making and responsibility	Somatic symptoms
Discrepancy between husband's and wife's earnings	Responsibility for the housework	Dysphoric symptoms
		Total symptoms
Wife's perception of the importance of her job relative to her husband's	Responsibility for childcare	Marital satisfaction
		Career satisfaction
Age discrepancy		
Educational discrepancy		

Marital influence. Despite extensive criticisms (Heer, 1963; Olson and Rabinsky, 1972; Turk and Bell, 1972), the two most common measures of marital power (the capacity to affect one's spouse) or influence (the use of that capacity) continue to be who has the say in decision making and who performs domestic tasks. In this study respondents were asked to indicate on a 5-point scale (1 = I have all or almost all; 5 = my spouse has all or almost all) the extent to which they were responsible for making major decisions. Responses to this question formed the decision responsibility index.

Respondents were also asked to indicate on the same 5-point scale the extent to which they were responsible for various tasks around the home (household shopping, housework, cooking, car and home maintenance, handling the finances, laundry, yardwork, and care of the pets). Responses to these eight variables were summed and averaged to yield the home responsibility score. Responses to two childcare variables (responsibility for childcare and discipline) were similarly scored to form the child responsibility variable.

Table 6.2: *Factor Matrix for Two-Factor Solution to Health Symptomatology Scale*

Item	Factor 1 (Dysphoria)	Factor 2 (Somaticism)
(factor)		
(−) Headaches	.21	.30
(2) Digestive problems	.24	.63
(−) Insomnia, trouble sleeping	.23	.24
(1) Constant worry/anxiety	.68	.25
(1) Tiring easily	.49	.23
(1) Feeling guilty	.57	.14
(1) Feeling I just can't go on	.67	.19
(1) Crying easily	.59	.19
(1) Feeling lonely	.55	.11
(−) Feeling fat, gaining weight	.31	.12
(1) Lack of interest or pleasure in sex	.46	.06
(1) Feeling of worthlessness	.59	.19
(1) Feeling irritable or angry	.69	.16
(1) Feeling sad or depressed	.77	.17
(1) Feeling shy or self-conscious	.46	.15
(1) Trouble concentrating	.44	.17
(1) Feeling tense or keyed up	.60	.24
(1) Irrational fears	.45	.31
(2) Faintness or dizziness	.10	.47
(2) Stomach ulcers or colitis	.11	.53
(2) Chest pains	.07	.43
(2) Nausea, upset stomach	.17	.70
(2) Recurring diarrhea	.16	.54
(2) Chronic constipation	.14	.41
(−) Poor appetite	.12	.38
(−) Trouble getting your breath	.13	.32

Note: First a varimax rotated factor analysis was performed with 19 iterations, and two main factors explaining 36% of the variance emerged. Second came another varimax rotated factor analysis requesting the best two-factor solution. Factors were formed by including items which loaded above .40. The alpha coefficients are .89 for Dysphoria and .76 for Somaticism. The total symptomatology index has an alpha coefficient of .89. Dysphoria explains 28% of the variance; Somaticism, an additional 9%.

Well-being. Respondents were presented with a scale designed to measure symptomatology and were also asked about their marital satisfaction and career satisfaction. On the former, respondents were asked to indicate along a 5-point continuum (0 = not at all; 4 = very much) the extent to which they were "bothered" by twenty-six symptoms taken from the SCL–90 developed by Derogatis (Derogatis et al., 1974). A statistical procedure called the varimax rotated factor analysis was performed on these items and two main factors emerged. The first we call dysphoria, and it contained fourteen items. The second, called somaticism, had seven items. Table 6.2 presents a list of the items. Marital and career satisfaction ("how satisfied are you with marriage/career") were assessed on 7-point scales.

The Findings

Differences between Mothers and Others

Previous researchers have found that marital satisfaction, marital influence, and psychological well-being among women are affected by the presence of children (Blood and Wolfe, 1960; Centers, Raven, and Rodrigues, 1971; Gove and Geerken, 1977; Horwitz, 1982). The first step in our analyses, therefore, was to compare the mothers with the childless wives in the sample in terms of their scores on the variables assessed (table 6.3). Mothers earned on the average almost $2,000 more per year than the women without children. Yet the discrepancy between the wife's salary and that of her husband was greater for the mothers. Similarly, there was greater educational discrepancy between spouses with children than those without. There was no difference between the mothers and nonmothers, however, in the extent to which they valued their own careers relative to their husbands' careers. On the average, both groups rated their husbands' careers as somewhat more important than their own.

The two groups did not differ in the extent to which they were satisfied with their careers, but the mothers were somewhat less satisfied with their marriages. There were no differences in the women's symptomatology levels. The two groups did differ somewhat in terms of marital influence. While there was no difference in reported responsibility for household chores, the mothers, by definition, had more responsibility for childcare than those who did not have children. The mothers also exerted less influence over major decisions.

How did a woman's resources relate to the amount of influence and responsibility she had at home? When we looked at the total sample, only two resources really mattered: a wife's pay relative to her husband's and the importance she gave to her own career relative to her husband's (table 6.4). The more a woman earned relative to her husband and the more important she perceived her career to be, the greater was her share in major decisions and the greater was her freedom from responsibility for running the home. Responsibility for childcare was unaffected. No matter

Table 6.3: Results of Survey

Variables	Scale	Overall Mean	Mothers' Mean	Childless Women's Mean	t	df	Sig.
Resources							
1. Wife's earnings	Salary in dollars	23,408	24,768	22,493	2.28	484	p <.05
2. Pay discrepancy	Difference in dollars	6,329	8,837	4,680	3.43	536	p <.01
3. Perceived importance of wife's job relative to husband's	−1 to 1	−.12	−.16	−.10	1.34	582	NS
4. Age discrepancy	Difference in years	2.18	2.54	1.96	1.91	695	NS
5. Educational discrepancy	Difference in 1–7 scale	.32	.50	.23	2.51	719	p <.05
Marital Influence							
1. Decisions	1–5	3.04	3.11	2.99	3.08	573	<.01
2. Responsibility for the house	1–5	2.75	2.74	2.77	.86	557	NS
3. Responsibility for childcare	1–5	—	2.69	—			
Well-being							
1. Somatic symptomatology	0–4	.40	.37	.42	1.45	759	NS
2. Dysphoric symptomatology	0–4	1.09	1.14	1.05	1.62	762	NS
3. Total symptomatology	0–4	.86	.85	.86	.27	757	NS
4. Marital satisfaction	1–7	6.09	5.98	6.19	2.31	610	p <.05
5. Career satisfaction	1–7	5.28	5.39	5.24	1.53	751	NS

Note: NS = not significant.

how much the wife earned relative to her husband and no matter how important she perceived her career to be relative to her husband's, she retained primary responsibility for the children.

Table 6.4: *Resource Variables and Influence Levels among All Wives*

| Resource | Influence Variables[+] | | |
	Decision Making	Home Responsibility	Childcare
Wife's earnings	− .05	.06*	.04
	(765)	(765)	(325)
Pay discrepancy[+]	15**	− .11***	.02
	(754)	(745)	(315)
Pay discrepancy[+] When wife earns more	.18**	− .12*	.05
	(221)	(219)	(80)
Perceived importance of wife's job relative to husband's[§]	− .18**	.09**	.01
	(787)	(789)	(338)
Age discrepancy[‖]	.03	.04	− .05
	(788)	(789)	(335)
Educational discrepancy[‖]	.04	.03	.01
	(751)	(753)	(321)

Note: Numbers in parentheses are the *N*s for that cell.
[+] The lower the score, the more influential or responsible the wife.
[‡] The higher the score, the greater the discrepancy in the wife's favor.
[§] The higher the score, the more important the wife sees her career relative to husband's.
[‖] The higher the score, the greater the discrepancy in the husband's favor.
*p < .05   **p < .01   ***p < .001

Given that the women's power varied somewhat in relation to maternal status (table 6.3), we looked at the association among variables separately for the mothers and for the childless women. We conducted a series of regression analyses to allow us to look at the relative importance of the resource variables for the two groups. These relationships are presented in Table 6.5.

For the wives without children, pay discrepancy and perceived job importance continued to be important predictors of the relative equality of the relationship. The more they earned relative to their husbands, the greater was their say in domestic decisions and the less likely it was that they would have exclusive responsibility for household tasks. Perceived job importance also predicted decision-making power, although not responsibility for the household tasks. The more important she perceived her own career relative to her husband's, the more influence a woman exercised over major decisions.

Table 6.5: *Relationship between Resource Variables and Perceptions of Equality*

	Wives with children		Wives without children	
Predicting Household Responsibility	Beta	F	Beta	F
Career Importance	.28	15.23**	−.03	.37
Age discrepancy	−.04	.42	−.02	.12
Pay discrepancy	−.01	.03	−.12	4.83*
Educational discrepancy	.15	5.02*	.03	.59
Predicting Decision-making Responsibility				
Career importance	−.18	6.22*	−.16	9.56**
Age discrepancy	−.02	.12	−.04	.72
Pay discrepancy	.01	.01	.15	8.26**
Educational discrepancy	.10	2.34	−.02	.12
Predicting Childcare Responsibility				
Career importance	.09	1.64		
Age discrepancy	−.00	.00		
Pay discrepancy	−.17	.83		
Educational discrepancy	.08	1.45		

Note: For the career importance variable, the higher the score, the more important the wife views her career relative to her husband's. For the discrepancy variables, the higher the score, the greater the discrepancy in the husband's favor. For the household, decision-making, and childcare variables, the lower the score, the more responsibility the wife has.
*p < .05   **p < .01

For the mothers, the pattern was somewhat different. Pay discrepancy was not predictive. No matter how much they earned—even if their earnings exceeded their husband's—their marital influence was unaffected. No matter what their pay, most of the mothers had more responsibility for the children and the household than their husbands and had less say in major decisions. Perceived job importance was the single most important predictor of equality levels. The more a mother valued her own career relative to her husband's, the less responsibility she had for the house and the more influence she had in decision making. Responsibility for childcare, however, remained unaffected.

In sum, then, for the woman without children, resources outside the marriage, as indexed by pay and her perception of the importance of her work, enhanced her influence at home. The greater her occupational resources, the better off she was in terms of decision making and household tasks. In this respect then, the women without children resembled men in earlier studies. For the mothers, on the other hand, economic resources failed to enhance their influence levels. The most important variable was associated with their careers, but it was a psychological one: the extent to which mothers asserted the importance of their own careers relative to their spouses' was the best predictor of equality levels.

Influence and Well-being

We next examined the relationship between reported influence and well-being, looking first at satisfaction and then at symptomatology levels. As we expected, the influence variables are mostly unrelated to wives' career satisfaction but significantly related to their marital satisfaction (table 6.6). The more responsibility a husband assumed for childcare and household tasks, the more satisfied his wife was with the marriage. Contrary to expectation, the husband's dominance in decision making was also associated with greater marital satisfaction for wives. Turning to the symptomatology variables, we find that the mothers' responsibility for childcare was significantly associated with all of our measures. The more responsibility she had for childcare, the more dysphoric was her mood and the greater were her somatic stress symptoms. No relationship was found between decision-making responsibility or home responsibility and symptomatology.

Simple correlations can be misleading, however, because they obscure curvilinear relationships. To discover if there were such relationships, we divided the women into three groups in terms of their level of responsibility. In the first group were those who claimed to have little or no responsibility. Next were those who shared the responsibility equally with their spouses, and finally came women who had most of the responsibility. No relationships between well-being and responsibility for home maintenance emerged. When we turned to decision-making responsibility, however, it became obvious that shared responsibility tended to enhance a woman's well-being, especially if she and her husband had children.

Table 6.6: *Relationships among Influence Levels, Marital Satisfaction, and Symptomatology (all wives)*

Symptomatology and satisfaction variables	Childcare	Home	Decision making	Marital satisfaction	Career satisfaction
Dysphoric factor	−.16***	.02	.03	−.30***	−.24***
	(334)	(781)	(788)	(793)	(801)
Somatic factor	−.11*	−.02	−.05	−.16***	−.11**
	(337)	(786)	(793)	(797)	(798)
Total symptomatology	−.17***	.009	.004	−.28***	−.27***
	(331)	(771)	(778)	(783)	(795)
Marital satisfaction	.13**	.13***	.10**	—	.16***
	(339)	(794)	(792)	—	(799)
Career satisfaction	.02	−.0003	.06*	.16***	—
	(284)	(786)	(793)	(799)	—

Note: For the symptomatology and satisfaction variables, the higher the score, the more symptomatology and the more satisfaction. For the influence variables, the lower the score, the more the wife does. Numbers in parentheses are the *N*s for that cell.

*p < .05   **p < .01   ***p < .001

Probing the Causal Chains

The relationship between influence levels and marital satisfaction has implications for how we understand the association between shared power and symptomatology. Perhaps shared power enhanced health among women in the sample because it increased satisfaction, which, in turn, decreased somatic stress and dispelled dysphoria. We explored the explanatory power of the domestic influence variables above and beyond marital satisfaction by determining how much the health scores varied as a function of influence after variations in marital satisfaction had been taken into account. We conducted a number of stepwise multiple regressions. In the analyses, marital and job satisfaction were entered as step 1, the influence variables were entered as step 2, and the groups of variables were regressed on the symptomatology indices (dysphoria, somatic stress symptoms, total score). Separate regression analyses were conducted for the mothers and nonmothers.

Table 6.8 summarizes the results of these analyses. As expected, both marital and career satisfaction were important predictors of psychological well-being for the women in this study. For the mothers, shared childcare responsibility and decision making were both associated with well-being even after marital satisfaction was considered. Shared responsibility for decision making guarded mothers against dysphoria and somatic symptomatology. Shared responsibility for the children was also associated with

Table 6.7: *Relationship between Decision-making Responsibility and Symptomatology Levels*

Wives' Status	Little or None	Equal	Most or All	(F Statistic)
	Responsibility Levels			
All Wives				
Somatic	3.84[a]	2.54[b]	3.05[ab]	(3.62*)
	(51)	(648)	(79)	
Dysphoric	17.41[a]	15.06[a]	18.08[a]	(4.80**)
	(51)	(648)	(79)	
Total	26.25[a]	21.37[b]	25.01[ab]	(5.62**)
	(51)	(648)	(79)	
Wives with Children				
Somatic	6.00[a]	2.41[b]	2.19[b]	(8.56**)
	(17)	(244)	(42)	
Dysphoric	20.18[a]	15.28[a]	17.38[a]	(2.66)
	(17)	(239)	(42)	
Total	31.18[a]	21.28[b]	23.19[b]	(4.75**)
	(17)	(239)	(42)	
Wives without Children				
Somatic	3.21[a]	2.73[a]	4.29[a]	(2.85)
	(34)	(377)	(34)	
Dysphoric	16.12[a]	14.83[a]	19.09[a]	(3.36*)
	(32)	(373)	(33)	
Total	24.13[a]	21.45[a]	27.48[a]	(3.67*)
	(32)	(373)	(33)	

In any row, means with dissimilar superscripts differ at the $p < .05$ level by Tukey's HSD.

Note: The numbers are mean scores: the higher the number, the greater the symptomatology.

The Somatic score can range up to 28 and the dysphoric mood score can range to 56.

The numbers in parentheses are the number of women in each cell.

*$p < .05$ **$p < .01$

Table 6.8: Hierarchical Regression of Satisfaction and Influence Variables
on Three Symptomatology Indices

Variable	Women with Children			Women without Children		
	beta	R² change	F	beta	R² change	F
For the Dysphoric Factor						
Step 1						
Career satisfaction	−.17	.04	7.44**	−.25	.10	30.20**
Marital satisfaction	−.27	.11	19.96**	−.27	.07	33.54**
Step 2						
Decision making squared	.15	.02	5.39**	.01	.00	.03
Decision making	−.03	.00	.24	.05	.00	1.04
Home responsibility	.22	.02	12.13**	.01	.00	.10
Child responsibility	−.16	.05	6.26**	—	—	—
For the Somatic Factor						
Step 1						
Career satisfaction	.04	.00	.30	−.12	.02	4.81*
Marital satisfaction	−.18	.03	8.02**	−.17	.03	11.14**
Step 2						
Decision making squared	.19	.01	8.29**	−.03	.00	.21
Decision making	−.25	.05	14.31**	.03	.00	.33
Home responsibility	.11	.01	2.66	.00	.00	.01
Child responsibility	−.08	.01	1.65	—	—	—
For the Total Index						
Step 1						
Career satisfaction	−.12	.02	3.97*	−.24	.09	26.93**
Marital satisfaction	−.26	.04	17.04**	−.27	.07	32.56**
Step 2						
Decision making squared	.18	.02	7.82**	.00	.00	.01
Decision making	−.11	.01	2.98*	.05	.00	.93
Home responsibility	.20	.02	9.39**	.01	.00	.00
Child responsibility	−.17	.03	7.09**	—	—	—

Note: The variable "Decision making squared," computed according to procedures in Cohen and Cohen (1975), is included because
of the curvilinear relationship found earlier.

*p < .05   **p < .01

less dysphoria for mothers. Contrary to expectation, greater responsibility on the part of husbands for household tasks was associated with higher levels of dysphoria among their wives. For the women in childless marriages, the effects of the influence variables were inconsequential after marital satisfaction was considered.

In sum, then, for this sample, the more equal a woman's marital relationship, the more satisfied she was with her marriage. Marital satisfaction proved an important factor in her psychological well-being. For the mothers, the perceived equality of their relationship was an important factor in explaining their psychological well-being even beyond that which was explained by their satisfaction with their marriages. For the women without children, the equality of the relationship influenced psychological well-being only through the increase in marital satisfaction. It seems that equality in the marriage has more power in explaining the well-being of the dual-career mothers than of childless wives.

Among the dual-career women who responded to the Catalyst survey, numbering over 800, and living in all parts of the United States, we found both similarities and differences between those who were mothers and those who were not. The mothers experienced their marriages as significantly less equal than did the women without children. The equality of the mothers' marriages was unaffected by their earning capacities relative to their spouses'. The only factor that enhanced equality was the extent to which they believed that their careers were important relative to their husbands' careers.

Why do mothers have less equal marriages? Why don't economic factors enhance their positions as it does with nonmothers and husbands (Steil and Turetsky, in press)? And why, given the other differences, were the symptomatology levels of the two groups so similar? The presence of children was not associated with increased symptomatology. Rather, the presence of children was associated with the experience of greater inequality in the relationship. The link between perceived career importance and relative influence suggests that both groups, but especially the mothers, achieved equality primarily through a psychological belief in and assertion of their own deserving. The capacity to do this at home may have been buttressed by the psychological support the mothers derived from their professional roles outside the family.

How extensively should we generalize from the findings? Obviously, the sample was not representative of the American population at large. The women chose to participate in the study; they were not selected at random.

Virtually all of the women in the study were professional workers, but less than 20 percent of female workers in the United States in 1980 classified themselves as professional or managerial. Finally, over three-quarters of the women in the sample felt that they and their husbands were equally influential in making domestic decisions. This seems a high percentage compared to the overall population.

Would the relationships among resources, power, and psychological health demonstrated here be found among another, more representative sample of women? Probably. The limits on this sample ought to have made the demonstrated relationships hard to find because they restricted the range of the scores. (It is more difficult to show that differences in power affect well-being, for example, when the differences in power are small than when they are large.) That the relationships proved statistically reliable with this sample means they should be even more visible with a more representative sample of working women for whom, presumably, resources and influence would vary more than they did in this group. But, whether or not the present findings would be replicated in a larger, more representative sample, the pattern of results obtained here has implications for the study of multiple roles. Roles can bring resources, and the employed married women may have more resources than the housewife. Certainly, the former is likely to have more money than the latter. Additional resources such as access to information networks or the psychological ones we have suggested here may be less easily perceived but, as Cynthia Epstein points out in chapter 3, no less real.

A given role sometimes provides a woman with resources that help her function in another role; but the reverse can also occur. Thus, for the typical woman in the Catalyst sample, the role of professional worker may have enhanced her ability to achieve a relatively egalitarian marriage, but the role of mother did not. On the contrary, in terms of power and marital satisfaction, motherhood proved more of a liability for the woman than an asset. Investigators should attend carefully to the context of people's lives to see whether various roles have hidden costs or benefits for the fulfillment of other life roles.

Bearing in mind the importance of context, we return to Jessie Bernard with whom we opened. She was no doubt correct in her criticisms of marriage as an institution. It may have exerted a negative effect on women at the time that she made her observations because at that time marriage meant motherhood to the exclusion of other roles. As marriage becomes more accommodating to more diverse and egalitarian roles, its deleterious effects on women's psychological well-being may be diminished.

References

Bachrach, L. (1975). *Marital status and mental disorder: An analytical review*. Washington, D. C.: National Institute of Mental Health, Department of Health, Education, and Welfare.

Beckman, L. J., and Houser, B. B. (1979). The more you have, the more you do: The relationship between wife's employment, sex-role attitudes, and household behavior. *Psychology of Women Quarterly*, 4, 160–74.

Bernard, J. (1973). *The future of marriage*. New York: Bantam.

Blood, R. O., and Wolfe, D. M. (1960). *Husbands amd wives*. Glencoe, Ill.: Free Press.

Centers, R., Raven, B., and Rodrigues, A. (1971). Conjugal power structure: A reexamination. *American Sociological Review*, 36, 264–78.

Clancy, K., and Gove, W. R. (1974). Sex differences in respondents' reports of psychiatric symptoms: An analysis of response bias. *American Journal of Sociology*, 80, 205–16.

Crosby, F. (1982). *Relative deprivation and working women*. New York: Oxford University Press.

Derogatis, L., Lipman, R., Rickels, K., Uhlenhuth, E., and Coti, L. (1974). The Hopkins Symptom Checklist (HSCL): A self report symptom inventory. *Behavioral Science*, 19, 1–13.

Dohrenwend, D., and Dohrenwend, B. (1976). Sex differences in psychiatric disorders. *American Journal of Sociology*, 81, 1447–59.

Ericksen, J. A., Yancey, W. L., and Ericksen, E. P. (1979). The division of family roles. *Journal of Marriage and the Family*, 41, 301–13.

Gilbert, L. A. (1985). *Men in dual-career families: Current realities and future prospects*. Hillsdale, N. J.: Lawrence Erlbaum Associates.

Gove, W. R. (1972). The relationship between sex roles, marital status and mental illness. *Social Forces*, 51, 34–44.

Gove, W. R., and Geerken, M. R. (1977). The effect of children and employment on the mental health of married men and women. *Social Forces*, 56, 66–76.

Gove, W. R., and Tudor, J. (1973). Adult sex roles and mental illness. *American Journal of Sociology*, 78, 812–35.

———. (1977). Sex differences in mental illness: A comment on Dohrenwend and Dohrenwend. *American Journal Of Sociology*, 82, 1327–36.

Heer, D. M. (1958). Dominance and the working wife. *Social Forces*, 36, 341–47.

———. (1963). The measurement and bases of family power: An overview. *Marriage and Family Living*, 25, 133–39.

Homans, G. C. (1961). *Social behavior: Its elementary forms*. New York: Harcourt, Brace and World.

Horwitz, A. (1982). Sex-role expectations, power, and psychological distress. *Sex Roles*, 8, 607–23.

Kidder, L. H., Fagan, M. A., and Cohn, E. S. (1981). Giving and receiving: Social justice in close relationships. In M. J. Lerner and S. C. Lerner (eds.), *The justice motive in social behavior*. New York: Plenum Press.

Mason, K. O., and Bumpass, L. L. (1975). Women's sex role ideology, 1970. *American Journal of Sociology*, 80, 1212–19.

Olson, D. F., and Rabinsky, C. (1972). Validity of four measures of family power. *Journal of Marriage and the Family*, 34, 224–33.

Phillips, D. L., and Segal, B. E. (1969). Sexual status and psychiatric symptoms. *American Sociological Review*, 34, 58–72.

Radloff, L. (1975). Sex differences in depression: The effects of occupation and marital status. *Sex roles*, 1, 249–65.

Report of the Special Populations Subpanel on Mental Health of Women, the President's Commission on Mental Health (1978). Springfield, Va.: National Information Service, U. S. Department of Commerce.

Safilios-Rothschild, C. (1970). The study of family power structure: A review, 1960–1969. *Journal of Marriage and the Family*, 32, 539–52.

Scanzoni, J. (1972). *Sexual bargaining: Power politics in the American marriage.* Englewood Cliffs, N. J.: Prentice-Hall.

Steil, J. (1983). Marriage: An unequal partnership. In B. Wolman and G. Stricker (eds.), *Handbook of Family and Marital Therapy.* New York: Plenum Press.

————. (1984). Marital relationships and mental health: The psychic costs of inequality. In J. Freeman (ed.), *Women: A Feminist Perspective*, 3d ed., 113–23. Palo Alto, Calif.: Mayfield Press.

Steil, J., and Turetsky, B. (in press). The relationship between marital equality and psychological symptomatology: Is equal better? In S. Oskamp (ed.), *Applied Social Psychology Annual.* California: Sage Press.

Thibaut, J. W., and Kelley, H. H. (1959). *The social psychology of groups.* New York: Wiley.

Turk, J. L., and Bell, N. W. (1972). Measuring power in families. *Journal of Marriage and the Family*, 34, 215–23.

Weingarten, K. (1978). The employment pattern of professional couples and their distribution of involvement in the family. *Psychology of Women Quarterly*, 3, 43–52.

Weissman, M., and Klerman, G. L. (1977). Sex differences and the epidemiology of depression. *Archives of General Psychiatry*, 34, 98–111.

7

Mothers' Participation in Childcare: Patterns and Consequences

Rosalind C. Barnett and Grace K. Baruch

Because social scientists have, along with everyone else, assumed that childrearing is a mother's natural job, we have made little effort to examine the extent and pattern of maternal participation in childrearing (Goldberg, 1981; Lawson and Ingleby, 1974). Because we have assumed that caring for children promotes women's well-being, few studies have explored the relationship between maternal participation and psychological functioning among women. This chapter breaks with tradition and focuses on the mental health consequences of maternal participation for married women. Using data from a larger study of the consequences for children of parental participation in childcare (Baruch and Barnett, 1986), we examine whether the association between involvement in childcare, on the one hand, and well-being and stress, on the other, is the same for women who work outside the home and for those who do not (Bell, 1983; Kessler and McRae, 1981; Ross, Mirowosky, and Huber, 1983).

We also examine the consequences for husbands of maternal participation in childcare. When women enter the paid labor market, their husbands typically perform more childcare relative to their wives than fathers generally perform in traditional families (Crosby, 1984). Men's reactions to

The research reported here was funded by the National Institute of Mental Health (MH #34225) and the Henry A. Murray Center of Radcliffe College. The authors extend their appreciation to research colleague Jane Traupmann, to project secretary Kathie DeMarco, and to Brooke Cheston, Patricia Gagnon, Barbara Kraft, Eliot Kraft, Pat McLaughlin, Elena Perrello, Jim Pfeiffer, Thalie Price, Russ Quaglia, and Diana Taylor. Zick Rubin and Joseph Pleck repeatedly provided invaluable comments on previous drafts of this manuscript; Joseph Pleck also provided important methodological suggestions. We are grateful for the statistical advice and computing assistance of Erin Phelps and Valerie Lee.

the amount or proportion of childcare performed by their wives have rarely been studied, but some data suggest that the consequences of male participation in childrearing are much more positive when the man feels he has free choice about his participation than when he feels forced to participate (Lamb, 1984). Such choice may be rarer in dual-earner families. We examine to what extent men's psychological well-being and their feelings of stress are connected to the maternal involvement of their wives, both in families where the woman works outside the home and in those where she does not.

The Sample

Sampling

Participants in our study were the mothers and fathers of 160 kindergarten and fourth-grade children. Names were drawn from the roster of families whose children were enrolled in the public school system of a mainly white and middle-class suburb in the greater Boston area. At each grade level half of the children were boys and half girls; within each of the four groups thus formed, half had employed mothers. Maternal employment was defined as working at least 17.5 hours per week for at least three months prior to being interviewed for this study. Nonemployed mothers were defined as employed less than eight hours per week. All the families were Caucasian, two-parent families; the child was the natural child of both parents. The sample was restricted to middle-class families, defined as those in which the father's occupation was Class III or above on the Hollingshead Scale (1957). Data were collected from the fall of 1980 to the spring of 1981.

In accordance with school system requirements, families could not be contacted directly by the researchers. Instead letters were sent by the school to all families with a kindergarten or fourth-grade child. The study was described to parents as being concerned with how mothers and fathers spend their time with respect to paid work, family work, and other activities, and how their patterns are related to children's attitudes about the roles of men and women. Interested parents completed an enclosed response card and provided the project with their telephone numbers.

Families who responded positively were categorized into four groups by sex and grade of child; within each group the respondents were further classified by the mother's employment status. Potential families in each of the eight groups thus formed were assigned random numbers. Families were contacted by telephone in order of random number by a member of the research team, who determined the father's occupation. This procedure was used to fill all but two cells, for which insufficient response cards were received. The school system then granted the investigators permission to contact potential families by telephone; this procedure yielded enough families to fill the remaining two cells.[1]

Characteristics of the Sample

The average age of the mothers was 39.4 years; of the fathers, 41.1. Of the 80 mothers, 39 worked from 17.5 to 29 hours per week; 37 worked 30 or more hours per week; four had lowered their work hours below 17.5 between the telephone screening and the interview. The mean occupational prestige level of employed mothers was 47.6, which is the level assigned to a bookkeeper and to the owner of a real estate agency. The mean occupational prestige level of fathers was 55.78, the level assigned to an accountant and to a social worker (Siegel, 1971). The mean educational level of both mothers and fathers corresponded to a college degree. Mean family income was in the mid-$30,000 range for the total sample. Fathers' mean income was approximately $28,000; that of employed wives was $7,600, reflecting the high proportion of part-time workers among women, the lower pay scales for women's jobs, and the tendency for married women, especially those employed by their husbands, to underreport their incomes.

Six of the 160 families had one child; 87 had two children; 47 had three children; and 20 had four or more children. Only 18 percent of the families had at least one child under three years of age, 62 percent had at least one child between three and eight years of age, and the remaining 21 percent had no child younger than nine years of age.

Because the effects of maternal participation were examined separately for employed and nonemployed mothers, the two groups of families were compared on a variety of demographic and family structure measures in order to detect differences that might affect the findings. T tests indicated that the only significant difference was in fathers' income, with means estimated at $16,000 for fathers with employed wives and $29,000 for fathers with nonemployed wives [t (157) = 11.18, p < .001]. There were no significant differences in total family income, number of children, occupational prestige of the husband, or the number of hours per week he

1. Because of the procedure used, only an estimate of the response rate is possible; it was approximately 40 percent of those on the roster. For the same reason, differences between families participating and those refusing could not be studied but are unlikely to be demographic, given the homogenous nature of the parent population. It is possible that families in which fathers participated the least were the most likely to refuse, given the current social desirability of fathers' involvement.

worked. Unfortunately, since the main study was designed primarily to investigate fathers' participation in childcare, no measures of attitudes toward the female sex role were included.

The Survey

Procedure

Mothers and fathers were interviewed in their homes for approximately two hours by a team consisting of a male and a female staff member. In accordance with Russell's (1978) recommendation, parents were interviewed jointly about the extent of their separate and joint participation in childcare and home chores, in paid employment, and in other activities. Demographic data about the family were also obtained jointly. Each parent was then interviewed in a separate room by a same-sex interviewer to obtain data on marital and parental role strain and well-being. Finally, a questionnaire packet was left with each parent to be filled out independently and returned by mail; the packet included the measure of self-esteem. Each parent received $5 for participating in the study.

Measures of Mothers' Participation

We devised three measures of maternal participation in childcare. The first was total interaction time. Parents jointly used a chart devised for this study to indicate for five typical weekdays and two typical weekend days (one typical week) the hours during which the target child and each parent were at home and awake. They then indicated the nature of the child-parent interaction that typically occurred during each of those hours. Hours during which the child was at home and awake and one or both parents were at home were coded jointly by parents and interviewer for level of interaction. Three levels of interaction were described to parents:

Level 1: No interaction: "Parent and child are not involved together. Each is engaged in independent activity with no interaction."

Level 2: Intermittent interaction: "Parent and child each are doing their own thing, aware of each other's activities, and interacting periodically."

Level 3: Intensive interaction: "Parent and child are actively involved together, as in doing homework, playing a game, or being engaged in a project."

Parents reported only a small number of hours in which they were at home yet unavailable to the child (level 1 interaction). Therefore, level 1 scores were omitted from further analyses. Intermittent (level 2) and intensive (level 3) interaction were combined into a total interaction score for two reasons. First, empirical examination of correlation patterns showed that the combined variable was more powerful. Second, the distinction between the levels, although conceptually clear to both parents and researchers, was not a good match to real-life interactions. For example, conversations held while a parent was chauffeuring a child were experienced as intensive interaction yet technically were intermittent.

The second measure of maternal participation, called proportional inaction time, was a ratio score. We derived this score by dividing the number of hours the mother spent per week in intermittent and intensive interaction by the total hours both parents spent in such interaction.

Finally, we developed a measure pertinent to childcare tasks that was modified in pilot work from Baruch and Barnett (1981). For each of 11 childcare tasks, parents were jointly asked to estimate what percent of the time the task was done by the mother alone, by the parents together, and by the father alone (0-20 percent, 20-40 percent, and so on). The tasks included: take child to birthday party; take child to doctor/dentist; attend teacher conference; supervise personal hygiene; stay home or make arrangements for care when child is sick. In the scoring, a "1" was assigned to 0-20 percent time, a "2" to 20-40 percent, etc. The mean time mothers spent doing childcare tasks alone constituted the third maternal participation variable.[2]

We also included a measure of responsibility for the 11 childcare tasks. Responsibility was defined as "remembering, planning, and scheduling." Almost all mothers reported very high levels of responsibility; almost all fathers reported very low levels. Because of the constricted range, this variable was omitted from further analysis.

Measures of Consequences of Mothers' Participation

We considered role strain to be an important potential consequence of participation in childrearing, and we assessed four categories of role strain for each parent. The first category concerned perceived time and energy problems. Each parent rated on a 4-point scale (from "not at all" to "very much") the degree to which he or she was bothered by lack of time/energy for each of the following: family, work/career, self, spouse, and friends. Second, a set of open-ended questions inquired about work/family conflicts for oneself and one's spouse. Coding on a 4-point scale (1 = no conflict;

2. The three maternal participation variables were significantly but moderately intercorrelated. Total interaction time correlated .52 with proportional interaction time and .30 with childcare tasks. Between the two measures, the correlation was .43.

4 = considerable conflict) yielded a maximum of four scores: two for self
(my work conflicts with family; my family responsibilities conflict with
work) and two analogous scores for perceptions of the spouse's conflicts.

A third category of role strain variables assessed parents' satisfaction
with three indicators of time spent with children and on chores. Each
parent indicated separately whether he or she was satisfied or dissatisfied
with the amount of time spent with children and on chores; the amount of
time the spouse was spending with children and on chores; and the amount
of time he or she thought the spouse wanted the partner to spend with
children and on chores. Fourth, each parent's overall satisfaction with both
the spouse's work schedule and overall time allocation was assessed. Each
parent also rated her or his perception of the spouse's attitude toward her
or his own time allocation.

According to our conceptualization, variations in well-being could also
occur as a consequence of participation patterns, and so we included eight
measures of well-being. With respect to the parental role, fathers and
mothers rated sense of involvement with the child (7-point scale), sense of
competence as parent (4-point scale), and satisfaction, that is attitude
toward being a parent (7-point scale: 1 = very positive, 7 = very negative).
Three aspects of the marital relationship were assessed: overall marital
satisfaction (7-point scale), sense of equity (7-point scale), and evaluation
of how good a parent the spouse is (7-point scale).

Amount of Maternal Participation

As table 7.1 shows, mothers who did not work outside the home spent
significantly more hours per week (M = 49.03) interacting with their children than did employed mothers (M = 41.87). For purposes of comparison, the fathers in this study spent an average of 29.48 hours per week

Table 7.1: *Mothers' Participation Variables by Maternal Employment Status*

	Mothers' Employment Status				
	Employed (n=80)		Nonemployed (n=80)		
Participation Variable	M	SD	M	SD	T-test
Total interaction time	41.87	9.45	49.03	11.40	− 4.29***
Proportional interaction time	.58	.07	.63	.63	− 4.12***
Childcare tasks	3.47	.53	3.60	.50	− 1.65

*** p < .001

(SD = 8.07) in total interaction time. Fathers' total interaction time did not differ significantly by wives' employment status (M = 30.13, SD = 7.77 and M = 28.84, SD = 8.36, for those with employed and non-employed wives respectively). Relative to their husbands, nonemployed mothers spent significantly more time interacting with their children (M = 63%) than did employed mothers (M = 58%). There were no differences between the two groups of mothers with respect to participation in childcare tasks.

Role Strain and Well-being among Mothers

What are the psychological consequences of maternal participation in childcare? To answer this question, we looked first at the four categories of role strain and then at the eight measures of well-being. We first assessed differences in the average levels of role strain and well-being among women who worked outside the home and those who did not. More important than these average differences, however, are the observed correlations between the measures of maternal participation, on the one hand, and the measures of role strain and of well-being, on the other.

Role Strain

The employed mothers did not differ very much from the nonemployed mothers in terms of the average level of role strain. Table 7.2 presents the average scores for both groups of women on the many measures of role strain that we used. For only one of nineteen specific questions did the women who were not employed report significantly more strain than the women who were, namely, being dissatisfied with the amount of time their husbands spent on household chores. In contrast, employed mothers were significantly more dissatisfied with three items. They were more bothered about not having enough time for friends, and they perceived their husbands to be more dissatisfied with both the amount of time they (the mothers) spent with the children and with their overall time allocation.

Was there an association between maternal participation and role strain for the employed and the nonemployed women? Among the eighty employed women in the study, none of the nineteen individual items assessing role strain correlated significantly with the first measure of maternal participation, total interaction time. Proportional interaction time was only marginally associated with four of the nineteen role strain items, as was the measure of childcare tasks. The only strong correlation found in the sixty tests conducted was between childcare tasks, on the one hand, and a feeling of too little time for family, on the other ($r = -.31, p < .01$). Working mothers who perform relatively few childcare tasks are likely to feel that they have too little time or energy for their family.

Table 7.2: *Mothers' Role Strain Consequences by Employment Status*

Role Strain Consequences	Scale	Employed women (n = 80)	Nonemployed Women (n = 80)	T-test[‡]
Average Scores[†]				
Too little time or energy for:				
Family	1-4	1.97	1.78	
Career/Work	1-4	1.62	1.73	
Self	1-4	2.15	2.13	
Spouse	1-4	2.10	2.16	
Friends	1-4	1.70	1.49	p < .05
Role conflicts:				
Work with family for spouse	1-4	1.64	1.71	
Family with work for spouse	1-4	1.00	1.01	
Work with family for self	1-4	1.64	1.00	
Family with work for self	1-4	1.57	1.00	
Satisfaction with:				
Own time for children	1-4	1.46	1.52	
Own time on chores	1-4	1.29	1.39	
Spouse's time with children	1-4	1.48	1.57	
Spouse's time on chores	1-4	1.38	1.59	p < .05
Own work flexibility	1-7	5.82	—	
Spouse's work schedule	1-7	5.44	4.91	
Spouse's overall time allocation	1-7	5.03	5.14	
Perceived satisfaction of spouse regarding self's:				
Time with children	1-2	1.56	1.71	p < .05
Time on chores	1-2	1.51	1.60	
Overall time allocation	1-7	4.76	5.34	p < .01

[†] The higher the score, the worse the strain.

[‡] This column reports level of significance reached in T-tests computing the two types of women. A blank means that the scores of the employed women did not differ, statistically, from the scores of the nonemployed women.

Among the eighty women who did not work outside the home, the association between maternal participation in childcare and role strain was similarly marked by its absence. Only one of the sixty correlations for this group of women proved statistically significant. The more childcare tasks a nonemployed mother did by herself, the more dissatisfied she was with the amount of time her husband spent with the children ($r = -.38, p < .001$).

Even though the employed and nonemployed women differed in the amount of total and proportional interaction time they reported (table 7.1), they were alike in that the amount of childcare they performed bore virtually no association with role strain. Why? It seems probable that the nonemployed mothers expected to do most of the interacting with the children, so that an imbalance between them and their husbands in this area did not result in feelings of dissatisfaction. The finding for employed women is more puzzling, for one would expect that doing less childcare would relieve the strain of managing dual roles. Perhaps, they too expected to do most of the childrearing. Or perhaps the strain of multiple responsibilities was outweighed by the fact that greater participation meant not having to ask one's husband to do more than was comfortable for him.

Well-being

The women in the study generally appeared to be psychologically healthy and contented. There were no differences between the employed and the nonemployed women on any of the eight measures of well-being (table 7.3).

Table 7.3: *Mothers' Well-being by Employment Status*

| | | Mothers' Employment Status | | |
Well-being	Scale[+]	Employed (n = 80)	Nonemployed (n = 80)	T-test
General				
Life satisfaction	1–7	5.44	5.61	NS
Self-esteem	1–4	3.27	3.26	NS
Parental Role				
Involvement	1–7	6.11	6.27	NS
Competence	1–4	3.04	3.22	NS
Satisfaction	1–7	6.22	6.18	NS
Marital Role				
Satisfaction	1–7	5.91	6.14	NS
Equity[+]	1–7	3.92	4.01	NS
Rating of spouse as a father	1–7	3.46	3.46	NS

Note: NS = not significant.
[+] High numbers are positive end of the scale.
[+] 1 = partner gets a much better deal. 7 = I get a much better deal.

The associations between maternal participation and well-being, like those between participation and role strain, were generally weak among both groups of women. Only three of the twenty-four correlations reached statistical significance for the employed mothers (table 7.4). The more she interacted with the child relative to her husband, the lower her self-esteem. However, her sense of involvement in the parental role correlated positively with her proportional interaction score ($r = .27, p < .01$). The greater the proportion of time the woman spent with her child, relative to her husband, the more involved she felt with her child. Also significant was the negative correlation between childcare tasks and the rating of the spouse as a father ($r = -.46, p < .001$): the more tasks a mother did alone, the less favorably she viewed the father's performance as a parent.

Table 7.4: *Zero-order Correlations between Employed Mothers' Participation Variables and Well-being*

	Participation Variables		
Well-being	Total interaction time	Proportional interaction time	· Childcare tasks
General			
Life satisfaction	− .04	.11	.06
Self-esteem	− .05	− .21**	− .05
Parental Role			
Involvement	.11	.27**	− .02
Competence	.01	.07	− .06
Satisfaction	− .03	.16	− .08
Marital Role			
Satisfaction	− .04	− .02	− .12
Equity	− .11	− .03	− .02
Rating of spouse as a father	.01	− .17 ·	− .46***

Note: $N = 80$
*p < .05   **p < .01   ***p < .001

That is, there was an association between shared performance of child-care tasks and a positive view of the man as a father. This association also held true, although less strongly, among the nonemployed women. Among them, moreover, satisfaction with the marital role showed a consistent, if modest, connection with maternal participation. The more the woman participated alone in childcare, the less satisfied she tended to feel about the equity of the marriage and about how much her husband did (table 7.5).

Table 7.5: *Zero-order Correlations between Nonemployed Mothers' Participation Variables and Well-being*

Well-being	Participation Variables		
	Total interaction time	Proportional interaction time	Childcare tasks
General			
Life satisfaction	−.03	.10	.02
Self-esteem	−.10	−.05	−.17
Parental Role			
Involvement	.15	.03	−.01
Competence	.14	.13	−.01
Attitude	−.07	.10	.16
Marital Role			
Satisfaction	.01	.15	−.18
Equity	−.09	−.19*	−.18*
Rating of spouse as a father	.07	−.22*	−.28**

Note: N = 80
*p < .05   **p < .01

It is interesting that a high level of maternal participation had, for the women in our sample, more impact on feelings about the marital role than on feelings about the parenting role. Theoretically, the overworked woman could view parenting as the source of her condition. In fact, to the extent that women were overworked as mothers, they tended to criticize their spouses.

It is striking that both the employed and the nonemployed mothers in the study expressed few complaints overall. They reported little role strain and presented a picture of high well-being. Both the employed and the nonemployed women carried the major portion of childcare, yet neither seemed to experience the situation as burdensome. Perhaps an expectation of inequity means adaptation to it.

Role Strain and Well-being among Men

The mothers are doing fine, but what about the fathers? Feminists and nonfeminists alike have characterized marriage as an institution that benefits men (Bernard, 1973). Changes in traditional roles may in fact inconvenience and challenge men more than women. If so, the eighty men in our study whose wives worked outside the home might have shown more role strain and lower well-being than those whose wives stayed home. One

also wonders about the relationship between a woman's maternal participation and her husband's feelings of role strain and of well-being.

Role strain

The associations between male role strain and female employment are
strong but complex. When the two groups of fathers were compared on the
role strain variables, virtually no significant findings emerged. On only one
of the nineteen variables did fathers with employed wives, compared with
those with nonemployed wives, report significantly more strain. The former were less satisfied than the latter with the amount of time their wives
were spending with the children [t (157) = 3.61, $p < .0001$].

Differences between dual-earner and single-earner families emerge
when we turn to the associations between maternal participation and
paternal role strain. In families where the mothers worked outside the
home, several of the fathers' role strain variables were significantly associated with mothers' participation, particularly with proportional interaction time (table 7.6). The more time the mother spent, relative to the
father, in interaction with the child, the more satisfied he was with her
work schedule ($r = .44, p < .001$) and her overall time allocation ($r = .34,$
$p < .001$), and the more satisfied he perceived his wife to be with his overall
time allocation ($r = .40, p < .001$), although, interestingly, he perceived
that she was dissatisfied with the amount of time he spent with the children
($r = -.28, p < .01$). In sum, the more time she spends, relative to him, in
interaction with the children, the more satisfied he is.

Among single-earner families, the father's feelings of role strain were
not as strongly tied to the mother's participation in childcare as in the
dual-earner families (table 7.7). Only one correlation reached the .01 level
of significance: The more childcare tasks a nonemployed mother did by
herself, the less likely was her husband to complain about not having
enough time for himself ($r = .27, p < .01$).

Well-being

Husbands of women employed outside the home did not differ on any of
the eight measures of well-being from husbands of women who were not
employed outside the home. On all measures, furthermore, the men responded remarkably similarly to the women in the survey. What about the
associations between a wife's participation in childcare and a husband's
well-being? In general, mothers' participation variables had more frequent
and stronger correlations with fathers' well-being consequences than with
those for the mothers themselves. This pattern was particularly evident

among two-earner families. The strongest pattern of correlations was between mothers' proportional interaction time and fathers' well-being consequences. The higher the mother's proportion of interaction relative to
the father's, the greater his sense of equity, that is, the more benefited he
felt in the marriage ($r = .38, p < .001$). At the same time, there was a
negative relationship between a mother's proportional interaction time
and her husband's feelings about himself, both in general and in the role
of parent. More specifically, his sense of involvement and his sense of
competence as a parent decreased with her participation ($r = -.25, p < .05$,
$r = -.29, p < .01$, respectively) as did his self-esteem ($r = -.33, p < .01$).
Fathers who participated more relative to mothers thus benefited with
respect to these aspects of well-being (table 7.8).

The more total interaction time the mother spent, the higher was her
husband's rating of her as a mother ($r = .29, p < .01$). The converse also
occurred: the more the fathers did, the more critical they were of their
wives as mothers. Finally, the more childcare tasks the mother performed,
the lower was the father's sense of involvement with the child ($r = -.40$,
$p < .001$), and the higher was his rating of her as a mother ($r = .23, p < .05$).

Thus, the findings reveal that mothers' participation was associated with
both positive and negative effects on fathers: the more she participated,
the more positive he felt about the marriage and the more negative he felt
about several aspects of his role as parent and about himself in general.
It is of course possible that fathers who are low in self-esteem and in
their feelings about themselves as parents have wives who are more
participatory.

In single-earner families, the association between maternal participation
and the husband's well-being was less striking but still evident. Two of the
mothers' participation variables were moderately and negatively correlated
with the fathers' sense of involvement with the child (table 7.9). The higher
the nonemployed mothers' proportional interaction time, the lower the
fathers' sense of involvement ($r = -.34, p < .001$). The same relationship
was found for mothers who did more childcare tasks alone ($r = .39, p <
.001$); the more they did, the lower was the fathers' sense of involvement.

The most significant finding of this study is that the proportional forms
of maternal participation—that is, the amount of time mothers spend
relative to fathers in both interaction and childcare tasks—had the most
powerful consequences for fathers. These effects were most pronounced in
dual-earner families. With respect to role strain, the more proportional
interaction time an employed mother spent, the more satisfied her husband
was with her work schedule, her overall time allocation, and the amount

of time she spent with the children. Thus employed mothers' proportional interaction time acts as a barometer for their husbands' degree of satisfaction. The more she does relative to him, the more satisfied he is. This finding supports the conclusion of Yogev and Brett (1983) that fathers' marital satisfaction is associated with their perception of their wives as doing more than their "fair share."

Table 7.6: *Intercorrelations between Employed Mothers' Participation Variables and Role Strain in Fathers*

Role Strain	Mothers' Participation Variables		
	Total interaction time	Proportional interaction time	Childcare tasks
Too little time or energy for:			
Family	.04	.03	−.00
Work	−.07	−.16	−.07
Self	−.12	−.14	−.11
Spouse	−.11	−.13	−.13
Friends	−.04	−.28**	−.02
Role Conflicts: Self			
Work with family	−.21*	−.08	−.21*
Family with work	−.04	−.08	−.09
Role Conflicts: Spouse			
Work with family	−.15	−.18	−.25*
Family with work	−.15	−.14	.10
Satisfaction with:			
Own time with children	−.10	−.19*	−.07
Own time on chores	−.12	−.16	−.09
Spouse's time with children	.02	.23*	−.20*
Spouse's time on chores	−.19	.05	−.12
Own work flexibility	−.10	−.25*	−.26*
Spouse's work schedule	.08	.44***	.21
Spouse's overall time allocation	.15	.34***	.12
Perceived satisfaction of spouse regarding self's:			
Time with children	−.21*	−.28***	−.20*
Time on chores	−.23*	−.08	−.12
Overall time allocation	.25*	.40***	.12

Note: N = 80
*p < .05   **p < .01   ***p < .001

Table 7.7: *Intercorrelations between Nonemployed Mothers' Participation Variables and Role Strain in Fathers*

Role Strain	Mothers' Participation Variables		
	Total interaction time	Proportional interaction time	Childcare tasks
Too little time or energy for:			
Family	−.25*	.14	.03
Work	.05	.02	−.11
Self	−.19	−.04	−.27**
Spouse	−.05	.15	.13
Friends	−.12	−.18	−.13
Role conflicts: Self			
Work with family	−.09	.04	−.04
Family with work	−.03	−.01	−.17
Satisfaction with:			
Own time with children	−.17	−.10	−.05
Own time on chores	−.00	−.20*	−.22*
Spouse's time with children	.13	.20*	−.14
Spouse's time on chores	.05	−.04	−.02
Own work flexibility	.11	−.11	−.04
Spouse's overall time allocation	.10	−.06	−.11
Perceived satisfaction of spouse regarding self's			
Time with children	.00	−.16	−.14
Time on chores	.06	−.03	−.02
Overall time allocation	−.01	−.10	−.11

Note: $N = 80$
*p < .05   **p < .01

Employed wives who spend more time relative to their husbands in interaction and who do more childcare tasks alone perceive correctly that their husbands are satisfied with their work schedules and with their overall time allocation. Interestingly, among both groups of mothers, those who were highly participatory were critical of the amount of time their husbands spent with the children. This finding supports Pleck's recent conclusion (1985) that, in two-earner couples, the wife's family adjustment and well-being are related not to the amount of childcare and housework she does in absolute terms but to the amount her husband does. The nonemployed mothers in this study were also critical of the amount of time their husbands spent doing household chores. Employed mothers appeared somewhat less critical, or perhaps discounted their dissatisfaction in the interest of harmony in the marriage.

Table 7.8: *Zero-order Correlations between Employed Mothers' Participation Variables and Father's Well-being*

Fathers' Well-being	Mothers' Participation Variables		
	Total interaction time	Proportional interaction time	Childcare tasks
General			
Life Satisfaction	− .17	.02	− .01
Self-esteem	− .06	− .33**	.08
Parental Role			
Involvement	− .18	− .29**	− .40***
Competence	.05	− .25*	− .18
Satisfaction	.20*	.17	.01
Marital Role			
Satisfaction	.13	.07	− .11
Equity	.06	.38***	.12
Rating of spouse as a mother	.29**	.14*	.23*

Note: $N = 80$
*p < .05   **p < .01   ***p < .001

Table 7.9: *Zero-order Correlations between Nonemployed Mothers' Participation Variables and Father's Well-being*

Fathers' Well-being	Mothers' Participation Variables		
	Total interaction time	Proportional interaction time	Childcare tasks
General			
Life satisfaction	.12	.11	.00
Self-esteem	− .00	− .17	− .14
Parental Role			
Involvement	.13	− .34***	− .39***
Competence	.17	− .16	− .19*
Satisfaction	.06	− .02	− .11
Marital Role			
Satisfaction	.02	.11	− .16
Equity	.12	.21*	− .03
Rating of spouse as a mother	− .04	.10	.09

Note: $N = 80$
*p < .05   ***p < .001

With respect to well-being, the effects on fathers of mothers' childcare participation were more pronounced than for mothers and were both negative and positive. Here again, the proportional forms of participation had more powerful effects. The more time a mother spent relative to her husband in interaction, and the more childcare tasks she did alone, the lower were his self-esteem and sense of involvement with the child, but the more benefited he felt in the marriage. The same pattern of findings emerged among fathers with nonemployed wives. Perhaps fathers who are not participatory are responding to conflicting pressures. On the one hand, they may enjoy certain traditional benefits in their marriages; on the other, they may have doubts about how well they are fulfilling new expectations associated with the role of father.

For employed mothers, proportional interaction time was associated with a higher sense of involvement with the child; performing childcare tasks alone was associated with lower ratings of spouses as fathers. The negative effects of mothers' participation on the marital role were somewhat more pronounced among nonemployed mothers. These women may be especially sensitive and vulnerable about the value of their maternal role and may interpret their husbands' relative lack of participation as a sign of devaluation. In a previous study (Baruch, Barnett, and Rivers, 1985), the well-being of nonemployed women, but not that of employed women, was associated with husbands' participation in family work.

Thus, for fathers, increased participation by the mothers was associated with decrements in feelings in the role of parent but gains in assessments of the marriage. The opposite pattern emerged among mothers. Increased maternal participation was associated with more positive feelings in the role of mother and less positive feelings in the marital role.

References

Baruch, G. K., and Barnett, R. C. (1981). Fathers' participation in the care of their pre-school children. *Sex Roles*, 7, 1043–54.

———. (1986). Consequences of fathers' participation in family work: Parents' role strain and well-being. *Journal of Personality and Social Psychology*, 51, 983-92.

Baruch, G. K., Barnett, R. C., and Rivers, C. (1985). *Lifeprints: New patterns of love and work for today's woman*. New York: Signet.

Bell, D. (1983). *Being a man: The paradox of masculinity*. Lexington, Mass.: Lewis.

Bernard, J. (1973). *The future of marriage*. New York: Bantam Books.

Crosby, F. (1984). Job satisfaction and domestic life. In M. D. Lee and R. N. Kunango (eds.), *Management of work and personal life*. New York: Praeger.

Goldberg, R. J. (1981). Adapting time budget methodology for child development research: Effects of family variables on allocation of time to child rearing activities and developmental outcomes. Paper presented at the Meeting of the Society for Research in Child Development, Boston, April.

Hollingshead, A. (1957). *Two-factor index of social position*. New Haven: Yale University Press.

Kessler, R., and McRae, J. A., Jr. (1981). Trends in the relationship between sex and psychological distress: 1957–1976. *American Sociological Review*, 46, 443–52.

Lamb, M. E. (1984). Consequences of paternal involvement. In J. A. Levine, J. H. Pleck, M. E. Lamb, and D. G. Klinman (eds.), *The future of fatherhood*.

Lawson, A., and Ingleby, J. D. (1974). Daily routines of pre-school children: Effects of age, birth order, sex and social class, and developmental correlates. *Psychological Medicine*, 4, 399–415.

Pleck, J. H. (1985). The consequences of "role overload." In J. H. Pleck (ed.), *Working wives, working husbands*. New York: Sage.

Ross, C., Marowosky, J., and Huber, J. (1983). Dividing work, sharing work, and in-between: marriage patterns and depression. *American Sociological Review*, 48, 809–23.

Russell, G. (1978). The father role and its relation to masculinity, femininity, and androgyny. *Child Development*, 49, 1174–81.

Siegel, P. M. (1971). Prestige in the American occupational structure. Ph.D. diss., University of Chicago.

Yogev, S., and Brett, J. (1983). Perceptions of the division of housework and child-care and marital satisfaction. Evanston, Ill.: Center for Urban Affairs and Policy Research, Northwestern University.

8

Men and Their Wives' Work

Robert S. Weiss

There is much research to attest to the emotional importance
to women of employment outside their homes—to the value of "multiple
roles" (Baruch, Barnett, and Rivers, 1983). But what is the meaning to their
husbands of such employment? Are husbands happy to have their wives
work outside their homes, grudging in their acceptance, or indifferent? Do
they view their wives' paid employment as an activity no different in its
essentials or its implications from their own or as some other, lesser, thing?

Joseph H. Pleck (1983), on the basis of an exhaustive review of research,
reports that men whose wives are employed do not appreciably increase
the time they give to home maintenance, childcare, and other familial
activities. They perform a larger proportion of familial tasks than is performed by men whose wives are not employed; but this is because their
wives do less, not because the men do more. This suggests that men do not
revise their assumptions regarding the distribution of marital responsibilities when their wives become employed. How, then, do they understand
their wives working?

This chapter is based on information from a study of occupationally
successful men. My colleagues and I conducted six to twelve hours of
interviews with each of seventy men chosen randomly from the street lists
of four upper-income Boston suburbs. The only restrictions placed on
eligibility for our sample were that respondents be aged between thirty-
five and fifty-five and that they occupy what seemed to be prestigious
positions in business or administration. About 75 percent of those con-

Copyright © 1987 by Robert S. Weiss. Published by permission. I would like to acknowledge
the helpful comments on an earlier draft of this paper provided by Carolyn Bruse and Sharon
Spector. Support for the work reported here provided by NIMH, Grant Nos. MH 36708 and
MH 39353.

tacted agreed to participate in the study.

We also conducted six to twelve hours of interviews with the wives of twelve of the men in the sample and interviewed both partners of an additional eight couples who lived in an upper-income neighborhood of central Boston. The husbands in these couples were in the same age group and occupational category as the men in our suburban sample. In these inner city families, more than in the suburban families, the wives tended to have careers, not just jobs. (See also Weiss, 1985.)

In all but one or two instances, including the dual-career inner-city couples, the men seemed to maintain traditional assumptions of marital responsibilities. These included the following:

- The husband is responsible for the provision of income.
- The wife is responsible for childcare and home maintenance, except that certain home-centered chores may be the husband's, including those that require mechanical skills or skills associated with the building trades, those that are performed on the outside of the home, or those that require physical strength.
- Husband and wife are each obligated to foster the other's well-being and the well-being of the children.
- The husband is the partner ultimately responsible for the protection of the family from external threat.
- Each partner will help in the other's domain of responsibility. The actual amount of help provided will be decided by weighing the need of the one to be helped against the time and energy of the helper. Helping out can be offered freely or can be a matter of negotiation.

This understanding of the partnership agreement of marriage is very close to English common-law expectations of marital partners (Weitzman, 1981:2-3), in which the husband is head of the household and responsible for support and the wife is responsible for domestic services and childcare. The men's understandings differ from common-law expectations in only two ways: first, they believe that the husbands' and wives' obligations also include a responsibility to help each other, subject to negotiation; and second, most of the men subscribe to a less hierarchical view than that implied by the common law. While the common law states that "the husband is head of the household," these men appear to believe that marriage is more nearly a partnership of equals, albeit one in which the man is the partner ultimately responsible for the provision of income and for the family's protection.

Whether the understandings brought to their marriages by their wives were the same as those of the husbands, we cannot say with confidence. Interviews with wives suggested that in many respects they were. However, one basis for marital quarrels could be a husband's refusal to accept a home maintenance chore as a responsibility, even though he was willing to help out by performing it. In these cases, the husband's stand might be "I'm happy to help out if she'll tell me what to do"; the wife's might be, "I don't want to have the responsibility of having to tell him what to do."

The clearest expression of traditional understandings occurs in households in which the wife does not work. Mr. Orcutt is in middle management in a public utility. He and his wife have two children of school age and one not yet of school age. His wife is not employed outside the home. Mr. Orcutt explained how they had arrived at their division of labor.

> I rely on Myra to make sure I've got plenty of clean shirts. I would say Myra relies on me to fix things, keep the cars going, keep the house going. Bring the paycheck home, I guess, would be the biggest thing.
>
> I don't think we ever sat down to say, you'll do this and I'll do that. Right off the bat, Myra was the cook. I never tried my hand at it. If I had to depend on myself to feed myself I'd probably starve. The week that Myra was in the hospital with a leg fracture it was Burger King, pizza, and sub sandwiches.
>
> When Myra was in the hospital I learned how to run the washing machine and dryer. And then for three or four weeks she was home immobile with a cast on her leg, so I sort of had to take over.
>
> Almost anything, whatever the need is, I'm there. The shade just fell off the roller; put it back on the roller. The other night Myra turned the garbage disposal on and it stopped. Well, it blew a fuse.
>
> We do things within our limits of capability. I put the new heating system in. I don't think Myra could have done that.

In the Orcutts' implementation of the rule of helping out, Mr. Orcutt does a good deal around the house. But it is important to note that so long as the tasks are in his wife's domain, it is up to her to give him assignments.

> As far as washing dishes, vacuuming floors, washing floors, we both do that. We both wash windows, we both rake leaves. Not always at the same time. Like this dinner that we had for twelve people, it's a lot of preparation work ahead of time, and as Myra is getting the food ready I may be waxing the kitchen floor or vacuuming.
>
> Myra might say, "Gee, if you have a minute, could you...?" or I might

say, "All right, what else can I do? There's no clear-cut division of you do this and I do this. There are certain jobs within our limits of capability that we each do individually. But these other jobs, I'll do it. And the kids will pitch in.

There are many jobs where she is very helpful to me. I'm putting up a ceiling. There are certain jobs that require another pair of hands. I'll be in the middle of something and I can't do it with only two hands, so she is around. Or if one of the kids is around, well, the older one is pretty helpful.

Men do not modify their understandings of marital responsibilities when their wives are employed outside their homes. They may well accept a lower standard of housekeeping or, with less good grace, less attention to the children. They may also accept that they must help out more (although Pleck [1983] found that, while men believe they help out more, diary records show that they do not). In any event, they continue to believe that housekeeping and childcare are their wives' responsibilities. Another of our respondents, Mr. Brewer, has a highly successful catering service. His wife works with him about twenty hours a week taking orders and doing bookkeeping.

Along with working, she keeps the house up and does the shopping and keeps everything rolling inside. I try to get everything outside, the repairs, things like that, paying the bills. She takes care of the household end—the food and the wash and whatever needs to be cleaned. Even though I try to help her out once in a while, I haven't been successful lately.

There are many variations on this basic model, to be sure. One respondent, whose wife has a full-time job, notes that he participates in fetching things for the dinner table. He also says that he is the one who makes coffee.

My wife does the meal preparation, but it's as likely as not that I'll get up from the table to add something or do something for myself rather than ask for it. Since I am probably the greater coffee drinker, I'll almost always do it.

A few men say they are more concerned than are their wives with neatness and so will take it on themselves to clean a room or to straighten up the house when guests are expected. But these instances of husbands doing household chores seemed, at most, minor modifications of basic understandings. In at least one instance, in which a husband did laundry, it was a way of behaviorally criticizing his wife for not having done it sooner—and his wife reacted with defensiveness and anger.

The traditional understandings seem to hold even when the wife has a career and not just a job. Mr. Foster is a highly successful lawyer; his wife earns a small but still substantial salary as a C.P.A. in a large accounting firm.

> We have separate bank accounts. Paula can sign on mine; I can't sign on hers. We've always had separate bank accounts. I used to give her money before she went to work.
>
> Paula buys the groceries. There's a guy who comes once a week with the groceries—that's a pretty good bill. And she pays for the house-keeping. And I pay for essentially everything else. I pay for the tele-phone and the light and tuitions and insurance. She buys a lot of stuff for the house that she wants to buy. Large furniture, that gets in a gray area. If we go to dinner, I pay. Generally. If I have money.
>
> Certainly Paula's working has made a very big difference in what we could do. But I have become the court of last resort. I mean, I'm the backstop.

Before Mrs. Foster returned to work, Mr. Foster's income supported the family. Now, although Mr. Foster is no longer his family's sole source of support, he remains ultimately responsible. Mrs. Foster pays bills in her domain of home maintenance, but he is, as he puts it, "the court of last resort." Mr. Foster makes his checking account available to his wife; he does not have access to hers.

The set of traditional understandings I have listed seem entirely accept-able to male respondents. They take pride in their responsibility for their family's support. Rarely do they object to their wives' being responsible for housework, although they do at times regret not having more influence over their children's care. When they disagree with their wives' approach to childraising, as they sometimes do, they can feel frustrated by their impotence to change things or sadly resigned to its inevitability. One re-spondent, at work an effective manager, exemplified the way men acceded to their wives' childraising styles.

> I tend to go along with the wife's beliefs and desires in terms of what those kids should have and what would be good for them. I'm a peacemaker. If I don't think that things are extremely wrong—and I don't find too many that are—or if I don't really feel all that strongly

about them one way or the other, it's more comfortable for me to go along with it. I figure that life is too short to fight everything.

Given their persistent view that providing the family income is a male responsibility, how do the men in our study understand their wives' working? In general they assimilate their wives' employment to their assumptions about how the marital partnership should work. Insofar as the income from their wives' work is helpful to the family, they see it as a matter of their wives helping out—analogous to their own contributions to home maintenance. But they also may view their wives' working as important for their wives' development or mental health. In this case they understand their own support of their wives' working as a contribution to their wives' well-being. And fostering their wives' well-being is one of their marital responsibilities.

We asked the head of a growing high-tech firm how he would react if his wife wanted to go to work. He and his wife have small children and his wife is currently full-time at home. He believes that if she did go to work, he would have to share more of the responsibility for childcare and this would be a burden for him. But, if she really wanted to work and if this would make her happier, then it would be his responsibility as a husband to support her.

> If my wife went to work, it would mean that she would not have the time to do all the things she currently does, and so she would obviously try to move some of those things to me, at some level. Right now we have one daughter in grade school and one daughter in pre-school. I suspect that we'd have to bring in some additional people to help raise the children when she's not there and I'm not there. And that probably would be a joint responsibility. And we'd probably have to have other people do some things she normally was doing. It's not consistent with my traditional values, where I think it's nice when the children come home from school that they have a mother there. And that's what I would, philosophically, prefer. But if that wasn't best for my wife and I realized it wasn't going to work, then I would let her do what she wants to do.

Mr. Foster took just this position when actually faced by his wife's need to work. Mr. Foster's wife, at home full-time with their three children, began to display depressive symptoms. After a while he decided that his wife's malaise resulted from her lack of an occupation she could herself value. He strongly supported her desire to return to school to do advanced work in accounting, even though it would mean more work for himself.

That time she was at home trying to deal with kids, I think that was probably the hardest part of our marriage. She was just restless, very restless and not feeling very accomplished. She was having a difficult time coping with being married and having kids and not having a career and being away from her family and just generally moving on into life. At least that was my analysis.

We never got to the point of having any help, or anything along those lines. But it sure was difficult. And we weren't able to talk very much about it, because it wasn't very well defined. But these were problems that were festering in there. She wasn't very happy, and that's about it. She just wasn't very happy.

Looking back on it, I think that I would really say she was pretty disturbed. I remember now, the way she woke up crying a couple of times, like in bed, talking about her life. I used to get bored with it all. I'd say, "Just relax and go to sleep," that kind of thing. It was just sort of unarticulated anxiety on her part, a lot of self-doubt. And I remember it was very repetitive and it kept going around in circles. And she didn't quite know what was bugging her, but something sure as hell was bugging her. I was trying to be supportive. Trying to make it work.

And what we did, she went back to school. I was absolutely supportive of her going back to school. Absolutely! More than supportive. I pushed it. Because, why the hell shouldn't she? Why should she stay home? It's ridiculous. Her working, I don't think, has affected me very much at all. I've done just about what I would have done before. I did the dishes before. I'll do whatever has to be done around here. I always have. My kids do. I don't want to get waited on. Not that she would!

I think what's been harder for me than it's been for her is when she was a housewife it was the natural thing to do entertaining. But as soon as she started to go to school, that aspect of our lives kind of passed away. And I'm a very gregarious person. I've got lots of friends and I do like to entertain and like to see people. It's not easy. But that's not a big deal.

It should be noted that Mr. Foster and his wife have a good deal of household help—he is not taking over as much housekeeping as his comments may suggest. Still, there are sacrifices for him in his wife's working, especially in her lessened availability as someone to facilitate his social life. Nevertheless, he believes it would have been wrong had he not supported his wife's desire to be out of the house, working in a field she cares about.

Mr. Foster thus views his wife's employment as something he has done for her rather than something she is doing for him and the family. His employment, in contrast, is important not only for him but also for the family. His income permits him to guarantee that the family will have the money it needs. But his wife's work is important for her alone—although, to be sure, her extra income is a help. By supporting his wife's work, Mr. Foster sees himself as unselfishly fulfilling his responsibility to support her well-being.

> I think men who aren't accepting of their wives' working are probably pretty selfish. I know there are a lot of people like that. We spent Saturday night with a couple like that. He wants his wife *there*. Why the hell should she be *there* at his beck and call? Women are people too! And they have a right to life. Even wives are people.

One respondent, Mr. Williams, whose children were in high school and college, was pressing his wife to go to work because he thought it would be good for her, although she was herself uncertain. For him, as for Mr. Foster, the money his wife might earn was not important. He thought she would achieve greater self-realization if she worked.

For respondents who are not quite as affluent as Mr. Foster or Mr. Williams, the money their wives bring home makes a difference in what they can afford. If the children no longer require their wives' full attention, these men may want their wives to work to "help out" with bills—just as their wives might ask them to do dishes or put the kids to bed as a way of helping out. Mr. Ryder, a manager of a design department, is in this situation:

> When we got married, twenty-two years ago, it was the wife's role to stay home and take care of the kids. Which Elizabeth did. She made herself available when the kids wanted her. She was around. And she had a very nice relationship with both our children. She devoted time to it. She never got bored or anything like that. A lot of women go out to work because they get bored or they might think they are making a contribution to the world, but she didn't look at things that way. She was happy, essentially, with what she was doing. And I was comfortable with that. That was the way it was supposed to be. The man would go out and make a living and the wife would stay at home and take care of the house and spend most of the time with the kids.
>
> Then two things came together. In the first place, we no longer have any children at home. And in the second place, we will need money,

at least for a couple of years, to pay two tuition bills. Those two things kind of came together at the same time. And she is going to be working and getting some money to help us over the hump with the tuition bills. After the tuition bills stop or maybe after we have only one child in school, if she wants to work, fine. If she doesn't it is really up to her.

I don't have the kind of pride that thinks my wife shouldn't work. Especially to raise the kind of money you need for college, it seems a reasonable thing to do. I don't really see any reason why I should be out working and she should stay home, just enjoying herself.

Just as men insist that they be directed when they are in their wives' domain of home maintenance, they also insist that they be the dominant figure when their wives enter their own domain of income production. Men who have their own businesses sometimes want their wives to fill in for an absent employee or to take on temporary responsibility at a time of high demand. Almost invariably, in our materials, they put their wives in positions in which the wives' subordination is emphasized. One man, for example, had his wife's desk in a corridor outside his office. (His wife accepted this for over a year, then blew up.) A single exception in our materials is a wife who became the bookkeeper in her husband's business and was defined as a junior partner. While at work, she maintained some distance from her husband.

Mr. Stavros, president and chief executive officer of a manufacturing firm, is typical of the men who brought their wives into their offices to help out.

> When Connie is an employee at the company she has a different relationship with my secretary than when she is the president's wife. When Connie is at the company, if I want something done, I give it to my secretary and she might give it to Connie. She goes to Connie representing the President of the company and says, "You do it."

This arrangement seems rarely without tension. When men "help out" at home, they may bridle if their wives are peremptory about asking them to repair an appliance or run an errand. Although they view the home and the children as their wives' domains of responsibility, they want to be treated with respect when given assignments in those domains. The men are less aware of their wives' desire for respect when helping out in the husbands' domains. One respondent's wife, a skilled accountant, refused to continue to help her husband with his business because of the way he treated her there.

On the other hand, men feel themselves pledged to protect their wives from misuse by others. This protectiveness displays itself in relation to their wives' experiences at work. Mr. Foster's wife had done much of the work of making her department successful but was then refused promotion. One of the reasons given her was that she didn't need the additional income because her husband's income was so large. Mr. Foster was outraged on his wife's behalf.

> This is a textbook case, what went on there. People who don't have daughters or wives, men who don't have daughters or wives who have gone through this, don't believe it goes on! This was so blatant it ought to be written up. I can't stand those people anymore. I just absolutely see red! Just the hypocrisy of it! That's what it is, it's hypocrisy! A liberal firm, that's what it prides itself on being.
>
> They said to her,"You handle things and run things." And it was all going very well. And then she walked into this meeting and they say, "We don't think you have enough experience." And then they said, "You know, she doesn't need the money anyway"!
>
> She doesn't need the money anyway! It's unbelievable! But you have a situation where you've got this group of people that, what they really care about is their own jobs and their own staffs. And they don't really care about any common goal for the department.

At this point the interviewer asked Mr. Foster how he had reacted to the mistreatment of his wife. His first concern was to help his wife recover from her hurt. But then, thinking about what had been done to her, Mr. Foster said his reaction became one of outrage. This was his *wife* who had been hurt, and he wanted to do battle for her.

Another respondent, Mr. Layton, a manager in an insurance company, said that his protective impulses had made his wife anxious. Mr. Layton's wife is a vice president of a home sales firm and reports to a man who can be hot-tempered.

> She would tell me things about the things her boss did. Well, I knew her boss and "That is my *wife*!" I was ready to say,"I'm going to call him tomorrow and tell him off." It caused some conflicts there. She said, "Hey, don't you dare. Don't you dare. It means my career."

This is quite a different reaction from the one the men themselves receive when they come home to say that they have been misused at work. Then their wives ordinarily act to support the men's self-esteem, often by reassurance that the men can count on their continued respect. Men tend to be less supportive of their wives' self-esteem and more ready to do battle for them.

An extreme instance of husbandly protectiveness was reported by a respondent whose wife had been fired by the music school in which she was a department head, apparently because someone had decided that the school would present a better image if her position were filled by a man. Our respondent's wife, whom we talked with, said that although she was deeply hurt, she would not herself have fought the school's action. She disliked the administrators for their treatment of her and would have been pleased to be away from them. Our respondent, however, would not permit the administrators to get away with misusing his wife. He insisted that she take the school to court for illegal discriminatory behavior. She did, won, and was reinstated. Working in the school has continued to be unpleasant for her.

Somehow, in the midst of all this turmoil, our respondent's wife was able to continue composing music. One of her pieces won an important competition. Our respondent is proud of her.

Pride in their wives' achievements is common among our respondents. One, whose wife is a visiting nurse, after first complaining that her work took her away from their home, described with pride her management of a potentially suicidal adolescent. An accomplished and occupationally successful wife is, in a way, an ornament. The husbands could feel that by supporting their wives' employment they had helped to produce their wives' successes. It should be noted that our respondents were themselves sufficiently successful so that they were not threatened by their wives' successes.

Together with pride in their wives' achievements at work, however, some men resented having to help out more in their wives' domains of responsibility. There was great variation in feelings of this sort—much seemed to depend on the extent to which men felt that they had the time and energy to take on more at home while still meeting their first responsibilities to their own work. One man said:

How I feel about her working, I am really glad about the job. I think that she's got an interesting job and she is making it more interesting and challenging than it might otherwise have been. And I can see it reawakening feelings of competence and mastery. I think it is wonderful for her to have that interest, to be enjoying the job. And in the long run if she does well and makes money, that is good for the whole family.

She would be frustrated if I gave her a hard time about putting extra time into the job. But it never bothers her that *I'm* frustrated. Still, along with being frustrated, I want her to be happy.

It was putting some strains on the family situation. She got tired. She wasn't used to working and the mental and physical energy that she was putting into it. So she would be on the couch when I got home, watching the news and not physically unable but maybe psychologically too tired to get up and make dinner or play with our son or anything. So I would walk in the door and, bang, I would have to take care of all these things.

But we talked about it a couple of times, about how we would divide up the chores and that seems to be working out pretty well. I took on more of the shopping and cooking one night a week in addition to helping her out other nights on cooking. And on a whole host of little things.

Other respondents, too, display the same mix of feelings. They want to support their wives; they are happy for their wives if their wives enjoy their work and proud of them if they do well at it. On the other hand, they feel they are making do with a lesser contribution by their wives to the household. The men feel that supporting their wives' employment is one of the ways they discharge their responsibility to support their wives' well-being, albeit at some cost to themselves.

We have found that men's traditional understandings of marriage are in no way modified by wives working, even if the wives have significant careers. Men whose wives do not work and men whose wives do work share traditional understandings of the nature of marital responsibilities. Instead of changing these understandings, men whose wives work—and the great majority of our respondents' wives do—assimilate their wives' work to the traditional understandings.

This means that men view their wives' work as quite different in familial meaning from their own. Their own work is a way of meeting their responsibilities to their families. Their wives' work, while it may help pay bills, is in their view primarily a way in which their wives achieve a better life. Therefore the men feel themselves to be unselfish as they support their wives' employment. It is easy for them to feel misused when in addition to forgoing their wives' presence in the household, they are expected to contribute more to the household division of labor.

Yet, if men's understandings of how their marriages should function have not changed, the behaviors to which these understandings lead have changed greatly. Thus, men continue to understand themselves as responsible for helping out in their wives' domains—one of the principles of traditional marriage. Today, however, this is likely to mean helping with housework rather than simply taking care of the children for a while; in some instances, it can mean sharing of meal production or other tasks that were formerly reserved for wives. In general, the tasks men perform are much more accessible to change than are men's understandings of who is genuinely responsible for the tasks. Marriages that may at first appear to be highly symmetric (Young and Willmot, 1973) thus may on closer scrutiny turn out not to be symmetric at all—at least as far as the husbands are concerned.

References

Baruch, G., Barnett, R., and Rivers, C. (1983). *Lifeprints: new patterns of love and work for today's women.* New York: McGraw-Hill.

Pleck, J. H. (1983). Husband's paid work and family roles: Current research issues. In H. Lopata and J. H. Pleck (eds.) *Research in the interweave of social roles: Families and jobs,* vol. 3. Greenwich, Conn.: JAI Press.

Weiss, R. S. (1985). Men and the family. *Family Process,* 24 (March), 49–58.

Weitzman, L. J. (1981). *The marriage contract.* New York: Free Press.

Young, M., and Willmot, P. (1973). *The symmetrical family.* New York: Pantheon.

III. Social Roles and Social Processes

9

Multiple Roles and Happiness

Walter R. Gove and Carol Zeiss

"Overall, would you say that you were very happy, pretty happy, not too happy, or not at all happy?" This and similar questions were posed to 2,248 adults across the country in a survey designed to look at the relationships between gender, marital status, and mental health. The research questions that we then posed to ourselves featured these: If we categorize women and men in terms of the constellation of marital, parental, and work roles they occupy, which groups are the happiest? Which are the least happy? Are women and men similar in this regard? How does satisfaction with any of the roles relate to overall happiness among women and men?

To guide our inquiry we turned first to the growing literature concerning the effects of multiple roles on physical and psychological well-being. Traditionally, sociologists and psychologists focused on the problematic nature of multiple roles, arguing that more complex role sets produce stress (Coser, 1974; Goode, 1960; Merton, 1957). Recently, there has been a shift in focus away from the stressful and toward the beneficial effects of occupying different roles. Samuel Sieber (1974) articulated four types of benefits of role accumulation: role privileges, overall status security, resources for status enhancement and role performance, and the enrichment of personality and ego gratification. Steven Marks (1977) advanced a similar argument. Peggy Thoits (1983, 1984) outlined how multiple roles can provide individuals with a set of social identities which, in turn, enhance their sense of meaning and purpose and reduce feelings of anxiety and despair.

The empirical findings are, of course, less tidy than the conceptual analyses, but some generalizations can be made from the different inves-

125

tigations. First, role configurations typically differ among men and women, and men tend to occupy more roles than women. Second, while excessive role obligations can impair well-being, multiple role occupancy generally tends to enhance physical and psychological well-being among both women and men. Third, the quality of role occupancy is as important or even more important for well-being than the quantity of roles. How one experiences a role matters.

The literature leaves unclarified the question of whether women and men experience particular role configurations in a similar fashion. Certainly they tend to differ in how they experience the life roles of marriage and parenthood (Bernard, 1973; Rubin, 1983). Men benefit more than women from being married (Gove, 1972, 1973, 1979), but the quality of marriage tends to be more important for women than men (Gove, Hughes, and Style, 1983). Some researchers also propose that women and men differ in how they experience paid employment (Crosby, 1982, 1984). Men tend to have better jobs than women and tend to play the provider role—that is, to be the primary source of financial support for the household—while women are much more likely than men to hold part-time jobs. Given that the significance of any one role can differ for women and men, we wonder if specific configurations also differ in their relationships to happiness.

This study revolves around the question of role configuration, gender, and psychological well-being, the last assessed by self-reported happiness. The first part of our analysis looks at the relationship between role configuration and happiness. We categorize the women and men in our survey on the basis of three roles: marriage, parenthood, and employment. Each person is classified into one of twelve role groups depending on whether she or he is married or not married; a parent with children at home, with children who have left home, or not a parent; and employed outside the home or not. At the center of these analyses lies this question: do women and men resemble each other or do they differ in the role configurations that make them happy?

The second part of our analysis incorporates role experience. Specifically, we enrich our understanding of the relationship between marriage and well-being by taking into account, for the married respondents, how close they feel to their partners and, for the unmarried, how much they want to be married. We also fold into our analysis of the parental role how well parents get along with their children. Finally, we expand the view of employment by looking at the desire for employment as well as actual employment.

Sample and Instrument

Sample

The sample included over a thousand adult women and over a thousand adult men, using the national probability sample reported in Gove and Geerken (1977), which was designed to look at the effects of sex and marital status on mental health. In an effort to get sufficient numbers of widowed and divorced respondents (especially men), 11,397 households were screened. Two call-backs were made if no one answered. There was an 8.8-percent refusal rate at the time of the screening interviews and a 14.5-percent refusal rate after the household members to be interviewed had been randomly selected. The average interview lasted for 80 minutes. In all, the following *N*s were obtained: married, 1,225; never married, 442; divorced, 300; and widowed, 301. This procedure produced a stratified random sample including more widowed and divorced individuals, particularly men, than would occur in a simple random sample. As a consequence, unlike other national samples dealing with mental health, our sample contains a substantial number of widowed and divorced men and women. We interviewed a relatively large number of people living in somewhat atypical situations and thus were able to look at a larger number of role configurations than would be the case in most samples of this size. If the sample is weighted so that it is representative of the nation as a whole, the scores associated with the various marital statuses are virtually identical to those presented here.

The Happiness Question

Mental health used to be defined as the absence of mental illness. To the extent that people were free from anxiety, depression, negative affect, psychophysiological symptoms, manifest irritation, and so on, they were considered to be in good mental health. During the last two decades, mental health has come to be defined in terms of psychological well-being, which includes happiness, life satisfaction, and self-esteem (see Bradburn, 1969; Gore and Mangione, 1983; Gove, 1978; Style, 1985).

The larger study from which the data came included three measures of mental health—happiness, life satisfaction, and self esteem—and a composite measure of negative affect derived from a combination of depression, anxiety, and paranoia. We make use here of the happiness measure for methodological as well as conceptual reasons. First, unlike self-esteem, happiness is not related systematically to employment status per se. Sec-

ond, unlike negative affect, happiness shows no association with age, and
so it is possible to compare role combinations (some of which are more
characteristic of younger people and some of older people) without wor-
rying about the consequences of controlling for age in the statistical analyses. Finally, and most important, happiness depends less than any of the
other variables on gender. Because there are small gender differences in
reported happiness, it is plausible to attribute gender differences in particular role constellations to the ways women and men experience the roles.

Role Configurations and Happiness

Most respondents in the survey saw themselves as happy. Table
9.1 shows the percentage of women and men who claimed to be very happy,
pretty happy, not too happy, and not happy at all. If we convert the options
to numerical scores, with "very happy" given a value of 4 and "not at all
happy" given a value of 1, the women scored 3.22 on average and the men
scored 3.11 on average.[1] Only a few women and men described themselves
as "not too happy" or "not at all happy".

Table 9.1: *Happiness Reported by Men and Women*

	Women	Men
Very happy	38.2%	33.3%
	(421)	(379)
Pretty happy	49.5	48.3
	(546)	(550)
Not too happy	10.2	14.9
	(112)	(169)
Not at all happy	2.1	3.5
	(23)	(40)
Total	100.0%	100.0%
	(1,102)	(1,138)

Note: Numbers in parentheses are the *N*s for that cell.

How did self-reported happiness correspond to role configurations
among the women and men? Table 9.2 displays the twelve configurations

1. Given the size of our samples, the differences were statistically significant (eta^2 = .006,
p < .001). Controlling for income, education, race, and age left the figures virtually unchanged
($\bar{x}$ for the women = 3.23 and $\bar{x}$ for the men = 3.10) and resulted in a modest increase in
significance (beta^2 = .008, p < .001).

Table 9.2: Happiness by Gender and Roles

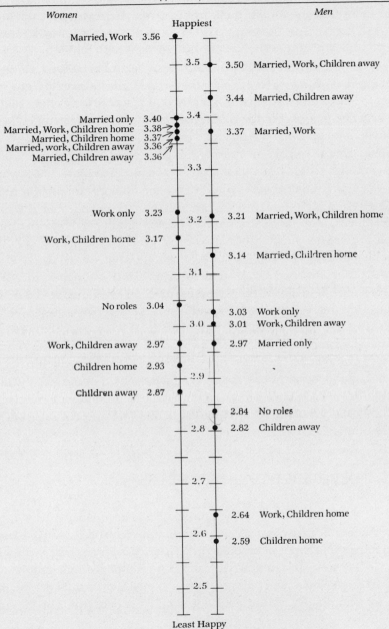

Note: No roles = None of the roles included in the analysis (Marriage, Employment, Parenthood).
Work = Respondent is employed outside the home.
Children away = Respondent is a parent, but all children have left home.
Children home = Respondent is a parent, and at least one child lives at home.

from highest to lowest for average happiness scores. Overall, women reported more happiness than men, and the married categories for both sexes rank higher than the unmarried. Four of the men's statuses ranked lower than any of the women's; unmarried men with children at home were particularly low on the happiness measure. For the women, all six of the married groups scored higher than any of the unmarried groups. Among the men, those who were "married only" scored lower than two of the unmarried groups, but the differences between the three groups were very small. Married women with children clustered tightly around the 3.37 mark, closely followed by the "married only" category. Employed childless married women scored highest for either sex on happiness $\bar{x} = 3.56$), while employed married men whose children were not at home topped the male categories ($\bar{x} = 3.50$).[2]

A few points appear clearly from table 9.2. First, for both men and women, the greater the number of roles, in general, the greater was the level of happiness. However, some role configurations were worse than occupying "no roles." Second, in some role configurations men were markedly less happy than any of the women. Third, for both men and women marriage was the variable most strongly related to happiness, followed by employment and then parental status. Finally, the relationship between marriage and happiness differed for men and women. For women, the six role configurations that included marriage were all associated with higher levels of happiness than were the six configurations that did not include marriage. Married men filled the top five happiness slots, but there was more variation in the degree of happiness across the different role configurations of married men.

Quality of Role Occupancy and Happiness

To understand how the quality of role occupancy affects happiness, we looked closely at role configuration, role experience, and happiness among four types of respondents: married women, married men, unmarried women, and unmarried men. For each of the four groups we examined employment and parental status as well as role satisfaction. All in all, we find that the nature and not simply the occupancy of the role matters.

2. To see if role configuration explained a significant amount of variance in happiness, we employed the Multiple Classification Analysis developed by Andrews, Morgen, and Sonquist (1967). We found that for men the set of role configurations explained a substantial amount of variance both before (9.0% of the total variance) and after controls (8.6%), and that the

Married Women

Married women in our survey were happier than unmarried women. But what happened if their marriages were not good ones? What happened, in other words, if the women did not feel close to their spouses? The same may, of course, be asked of employment and parenting. What is the impact on happiness if employed women do not wish to work or if housewives do? If mothers do not get along with their children, is this reflected in their happiness levels?

To answer these questions, we examined the associations between happiness and a measure of role experience among each of the six groups of married women (table 9.3). The third column indicates whether there was a statistically significant relationship between how happy a woman reported herself to be and how close she felt to her husband. In all six role configurations, these two variables were strongly related.[3] Among married women who had no job and no children, the association between reported marital closeness and happiness was especially strong. Compared to other married women, women who were "married only" were particularly happy if they felt "very close" to their spouse, but they were less happy than other married women if they felt "pretty close" or "not at all close." Among the married women, then, one of the benefits of multiple roles was clearly to buffer the consequences for overall happiness of dissatisfactions in the marital role.

The effect on happiness of role satisfaction was more complex when it came to employment. It usually did not matter whether or not a woman's actual employment situation matched her desired employment situation. For two groups of employed women (groups 1 and 2 in table 9.3) women who did not wish to work were as happy as those who did. Similarly, for two groups of housewives (groups 4 and 5) women who did wish to work were as happy as those who stayed home voluntarily.

---

different role configurations were much more powerful predictors of happiness than the control variables of income, education, race, and age. For women, the set of role configurations also explained a substantial proportion of the variance both before (7.7% of the total variance) and after controls (6.9%). But the set of role configurations was a somewhat more powerful predictor of happiness for men than for women. For women, unlike men, the control variables were also fairly strong predictors of happiness; income, education, and race are strong predictors at the zero-order level. After controls were introduced, the relationships of income, education, and race, although reduced, were still statistically significant, and age emerged as a strong predictor. Overall, the role and control variables explained slightly more variance for women (14.3%) than for men (11.7%).

3. The amount of variance in happiness independently explained by how close wives felt to their husbands was 15.2% before adjusting for the control variables and 13.9% after adjusting.

Table 9.3: Association between Happiness and Role Experience among Married Women

| | Characteristics of the Group | | | Relationship to Happiness | | | |
	Employment status	Parental status	Closeness to a spouse[+]	Employment status matches desire to work	Get along with children	N[‡]
1.	Employed	No Children	Matters	Unrelated	—	25
2.	Employed	Children not at home	Matters	Unrelated	Matters	30
3.	Employed	Children at home	Matters	Matters	Matters	122
4.	Unemployed	No children	Matters a great deal	Unrelated	—	32
5.	Unemployed	Children not at home	Matters	Unrelated	Unrelated	74
6.	Unemployed	Children at home	Matters	Matters	Matters	270

[+] This column shows for which groups closeness to spouse matters for happiness or is unrelated to happiness

[‡] Number in each group

Quite different was the situation for women with children in the home. Employed mothers with children at home were substantially less happy if they worked unwillingly than if they wanted to work. Housewives with children at home who desired employment were also much less happy than their counterparts who did not desire employment outside the home. Similar findings were obtained by Ross, Mirowsky, and Huber (1983). In their study, as in ours, it seems as if the one situation in which the employment of married women has been viewed as particularly problematic (namely, when children are at home) is the one situation where women's happiness depended on the correspondence between their desires for employment and their actual employment status.

How well a woman got along with her children was strongly related to her happiness if the children lived at home. This was true whether or not the woman worked. Among mothers whose children had left home, the quality of the relationship with the child mattered, but only if the woman was employed.

Married Men

The relationships between marriage, employment, and happiness were quite different for men than for women. How close a man felt to his wife bore a strong relationship to his happiness, but the association between marital closeness and happiness was not as strong among the men as it was among the women.[4] Furthermore, closeness and happiness behaved differently among the various role configurations occupied by married men. Unemployed married men, both those who had children at home and those who did not, reported less happiness than women in comparable roles. Among these two groups of men were a disproportionate number who admitted that they felt "not very close" to their wives. This suggests that men who were not providing financial support for their families experienced marital difficulties as well as low levels of happiness. While among women marital closeness and happiness were most closely related in those who had only the wife role, among men they were most closely related in those who were childless and employed. The combination of the two roles "married and employed" thus appeared to have a substantially different meaning for men than for women.

Among married men who were employed, there was relatively little relationship between happiness and satisfaction with employment status.

4. The amount of variance in happiness explained by how close husbands felt to their spouse was 10.1% and 9.9% before and after adjusting for the control variables.

Married men who were not employed reported lower levels of happiness than employed men, and unemployed men who wished to work were considerably less happy than men who were satisfied with their unemployment. Involuntarily unemployed married men, furthermore, tended to be less happy than their female counterparts.

Unmarried Women

While marital closeness was related to happiness among the six groups of married women, satisfaction with the single life bore no relationship to happiness for unmarried women. All unmarried respondents were asked how much they wanted to be married: a great deal, a fair amount, not too much, or not at all. Looking at each of the six role configurations among the unmarried women, no pattern emerged concerning the desire for marriage. The unmarried women who desired marriage were just as happy as the unmarried women who did not desire marriage.

Among unmarried women, employment was generally associated with happiness, regardless of whether the woman expressed a desire to work or to stay home. The one exception concerned the relatively few single mothers who were reluctantly employed. Such women were significantly less happy than single mothers who were willingly employed. A slight majority of unemployed women with children in the home indicated they wished they were employed, and these women were less happy than their counterparts who were satisfied with not being employed. The same contrast also held true for women who occupied no roles, although a smaller proportion of them desired employment. Most of the women who desired employment were of an age to be financially responsible for themselves and they may have perceived themselves as failures. In sharp contrast was the elevated happiness of women who expressed a desire to work but were unmarried and unemployed, with children who had left home. These women were of retirement age, and the counterintuitive finding makes sense if one sees their desire for employment as an expression of a relatively robust physical and mental state.

How well unmarried mothers get along with their children exerted an influence on their happiness in a fairly simple way. If the children were in the home and the mother did not work, the relationship with the children related quite clearly to the mother's happiness. Among employed mothers with children at home and among mothers with departed children, there was no association between the woman's self-reported happiness and how well she got on with her children.

Unmarried Men

The desire for marriage affected the happiness of unmarried men more than the unmarried women. The pattern of the relationships, however, was fairly complex (table 9.4). Among the unmarried men, the desire for marriage was tied to low levels of happiness for those with children at home, regardless of their employment status. The opposite association obtained among unemployed unmarried childless men and among unemployed unmarried men with children not at home. Since these groups of men tend to be elderly, the desire for marriage among men (like the desire for employment among retirement-age women) might have been an indication of good health and robustness.

Table 9.4: *Association between Happiness and Desire for Marriage among Unmarried Men*

	Characteristics of the Group		Relation to Happiness[+]	N[‡]
	Employment Status	*Parental status*		
1.	Employed	No children	No relationship	168
2.	Employed	Children not at home	No relationship	89
3.	Employed	Children at home	Negative relationship	41
4.	Unemployed	No children	Positive relationship	89
5.	Unemployed	Children not at home	Positive relationship	72
6.	Unemployed	Children at home	Negative relationship	18

[+] A positive relationship means happiness was greater among men who desired marriage than among others. A negative relationship means happiness was lower among men who desired marriage than among others.
[‡] Number in each group.

The correspondence between actual and desired employment status and happiness among the unmarried men was generally nil. Among only one group did satisfaction with actual employment status correspond to happiness: Unemployed men with children in the home were significantly less happy if they desired to work than if they did not. The average happiness score of the latter group was 2.88. The average happiness score of the former group was 2.30—off the bottom of the scale in table 9.2. The quality of the relationship between unmarried men and their children was strongly related to men's happiness. It mattered a great deal to the single fathers with children in the home, the most unhappy people in the survey, how well they got along with their children. In fact, the association between happiness and the parent-child relationship was greater among the single fathers than among the single mothers.

Role occupancy among the women and men in our survey was clearly related to happiness. Marriage was associated with happiness among women and men. So was employment and, to a lesser degree, parenthood. With several exceptions, the general rule was: the more roles, the better. While women and men resembled each other in terms of the benefits reaped from role accumulation, the two genders appeared to experience their roles differently. While the *fact* of being married proved more important as a predictor of male happiness than female happiness, the *nature* of the marriage mattered more for women than for men. How close a married man felt to his spouse was strongly related to his happiness, but how close a women felt to her spouse was a more powerful predictor of her happiness.

The meaning of employment also differed for women and men. Employment increased happiness for all women, regardless of their desire for employment—except for mothers (married or single) with children at home. Among these women, happiness depended on a correspondence between actual and desired employment status. If the combination of employment and motherhood sometimes proved problematic, the combination of unemployment and fatherhood also did.

Finally, the meaning of the parental role also differed for women and men. Men appeared happiest when their children had left home and least happy if they were not parents. In contrast, women were slightly happier if they were not parents. Married women were least happy if their children had left home, and unmarried women reported less happiness if they were parents than if they were not. The gender differences were statistically significant, but not strong. Among women and men, the better the quality of the relationship with one's children, the happier one was.

References

Bernard, J. (1973). *The future of marriage*. New York: Bantam Books.

Bradburn, N. M. (1969). *The structure of psychological well-being*. Chicago: Aldine Press.

Coser, L., with Coser, R. L. (1974). *Greedy institutions*. New York: Free Press.

Crosby, F. (1982). *Relative deprivation and working women*. New York: Oxford University Press.

———. (1984). Job satisfaction and domestic life. In M. D. Lee and R. N. Kunango (eds.), *Management of work and personal life*. New York: Praeger, 41–60.

Goode, W. (1960). A theory of role strain. *American Sociological Review*, 25, 483–96.

Gore, S., and Mangione, T. (1983). Social links, sex roles, and psychological distress: Additive and interactive models of sex differences. *Journal of Health and Social Behavior*, 24, 300–12.

Gove, W. (1972). Sex, marital status and mental illness. *Social Forces*, 51, 34–55.

———. (1973). Sex, marital status, and mobility. *American Journal of Sociology*, 79, 45–67.

———. (1978). Sex differences in mental illness among adult men and women: An examination of four questions raised regarding whether or not women actually have higher rates. *Social Science and Medicine*, 12, 187–98.

———. (1979). Sex, marital status and psychiatric treatment: A research note. *Social Forces*, 58, 89–93.

Gove, W., and Geerken, M. (1977). Response bias in surveys and mental health: An empirical investigation. *American Journal of Sociology*, 82, 1289–1317.

Gove, W., Hughes, M., and Style, C. (1983). Does marriage have positive effects on the psychological well-being of the individual? *Journal of Health and Social Behavior*, 24, 112–24.

Marks, S. (1977). Multiple roles and role strain: Some notes on human energy, time, and commitment. *American Sociological Review*, 42, 921–36.

Merton, R. (1957). *Social theory and social structure*, rev. ed. New York: Free Press.

Ross, C., Mirowsky, J., and Huber, J. (1983). Dividing work, sharing work, and in-between: Marriage patterns and depression. *American Sociological Review*, 48, 809–23.

Rubin, L. (1983). *Intimate strangers: Men and women together*. New York: Harper Colophon.

Sieber, S. (1974). Toward a theory of role accumulation. *American Sociological Review*, 39, 567–78.

Style, C. (1985). Chronological age and adult psychological maturation. Ph. D. diss., Vanderbilt University.

Thoits, P. (1983). Multiple identities and psychological well-being: A reformulation and test of the social isolation hypothesis. *American Sociological Review*, 48, 174–87.

———. (1984). Multiple identities: Explaining gender and marital status differences in distress. Paper presented at the Self-identity Conference, Gandiff, Wales, July.

10

Role Involvement, Gender, and Well-being

Lerita M. Coleman, Toni C. Antonucci,
Pamela K. Adelmann

A common finding in the social sciences is that women in general have poorer mental and physical health than men (Chesler, 1972). Some scholars, like Myrna Weissman and Gerald Klerman (1977) in their much-cited review article on depression, attributed the observed gender differences to biology. More recently, investigators have challenged the biological position, suggesting that differences in the mental and physical health of men and women may have been due to the kinds of social roles they have traditionally occupied (Aneshensel, Frerichs, and Clark, 1981; Cleary and Mechanic, 1983; Gove and Geerken, 1977; Verbrugge, 1983).

One important role that has been differentially available to the two genders is work, that is, participation in the paid labor force. A number of studies have, accordingly, examined the relationship between labor force participation and well-being among women. The findings have been inconsistent. Some researchers find no significant differences in the mental distress scores of women employed outside the home and homemakers (Aneshensel, Frerichs, and Clark, 1981; Cleary and Mechanic, 1983; Pearlin, 1975). Other investigators (for example, Gove and Geerken, 1977) find an advantage for employed women.

What accounts for the inconsistencies among the studies? Divergent

This research was funded by grants from the National Institute of Aging (1 R23 AG04285–01) and the National Institute of Mental Health (1 R01 MH38722–01). The manuscript was completed while Lerita M. Coleman was a fellow at the Center for Advanced Study in the Behavioral Sciences and she is grateful to the John D. and Catherine T. MacArthur Foundation and the Ford Foundation for their support. We wish to thank Joseph Veroff, Elizabeth Douvan, and Richard Kulka for use of their data; Susan Crohan for her helpful comments on an earlier draft of this manuscript; and Phyllis White and Deb Ottaway for preparation of the manuscript.

findings are quite probably due in large measure to differences among the populations studied by various investigators. Research investigating gender differences in mental and physical health roles often fails to take into account age and life-cycle period. Yet we know that involvement in work and especially involvement in the parenting role differ as a worker and her children age.

This chapter examines the associations among role occupancy, gender, and well-being at midlife. We perform secondary analysis on data originally collected in 1976 and pose two primary questions: First, do the women and men in the sample differ in terms of their physical or mental health and in terms of the roles they occupy? Second, what is the relationship between role occupancy and well-being among the women and among the men?

Sample and Measures

Sample

The data used to examine these questions were taken from a national survey of 2,264 adults (Veroff, Douvan, and Kulka, 1981), conducted by the Survey Research Center at the University of Michigan in the summer of 1976. The sample was drawn using area probability sampling methods to yield a representative sample of the American adult population, aged twenty-one years or older (see Kish and Hess, 1965, for a detailed description of the sampling procedures). From the survey 389 women (206 working, 183 nonworking) and 293 men (257 working, and 36 nonworking) between the ages of forty and fifty-nine were selected to represent a middle-aged sample for our study. In determining employment status, working was defined as any amount of paid employment outside the home (including part-time employment). Nonworking people were defined as those not working at all for pay outside of the home. Information regarding volunteer work was not available and therefore could not be considered in this study.

Of the 206 working women, 58% were married and 42% were not married (5% single, 16% widowed, and 21% divorced or separated). In contrast, among the 183 nonworking women, 84% were married, and 16% were not married (1% single, 10% widowed, and 5% divorced or separated). Among the 257 working men, 86% were married and 14% not married (3% single, 2% widowed, and 9% divorced or separated). The sample also included 36 nonworking males, 69% of whom were married and 30% of whom were not married (17% single, 3% widowed, and 11% separated or divorced).

Measures

Six indicators of well-being and distress were chosen from Veroff, Douvan, and Kulka (1981) as representative of a variety of psychological and physical health measures. These variables included: physical health, psychological anxiety, self-esteem, depression, immobilization, and perceived control. The number of items, range of scores, and a sample item for each measure appear in table 10.1. The self-esteem items (with minor differences in wording) were selected from the Rosenberg Self-Esteem Scale (Rosenberg, 1965), an index that measures the self-acceptance aspect of self-esteem. The depression scale consists essentially of the positively worded items from the Zung (1965) Self-Rating Depression scale. The physical health, psychological anxiety, and immobilization scales were derived from a factor analysis of a 20-item symptom checklist (Veroff, Douvan, and Kulka, 1981). The measure of immobilization was comprised of such items as "difficulty getting up or getting going"; "hands sweat"; or "prone to drinking," which stem from the anxiety associated with performance in achievement-oriented situations or from conflicts surrounding interpersonal commitment. Perceived control was measured by a single question asking whether the respondents felt they could run their own life or whether the problems of life were sometimes too big for them.

Other variables included marital status, parental status, education, and family income. Marital status was measured dichotomously (with 0 = not married and 1 = married). Similarly, parental status was a dichotomous variable (0 = not parent, 1 = parent). Education was measured as the highest grade in school completed, ending with 17 years or more. Income was defined as an eighteen–level family income variable ranging from <$1,000 to >$35,000.

Involvement in Multiple Roles

We began by exploring the distribution of women and men in the traditional social roles at midlife. The distribution of role constellations among men and women is an especially interesting question because our sample is, in fact, representative of the country at large. Most people in our sample had multiple (two or more) roles. Figure 10.1 illustrates that very few women and men at middle age were involved in no roles or in only one role. A small proportion of the sample (2%) participated only in the marital role, and no men reported being married only. A similarly small number of women (4%) were nonworking single parents; only 2% of the men were in this category. An equal number of women and men (4%) were involved

Table 10.1: Measures of Psychological Well-being

Measure	Items	Range	Sample item
Physical health	6	9–24	"For the most part, do you feel healthy enough to carry out the things that you would like to do?"
Psychological anxiety	5	5–20	"Have you ever been bothered by nervousness, feeling fidgety and tense?"
Self-esteem	3	3–15	"I feel that I am a person of worth, at least as much as others."
Depression	6	6–30	"I feel that I am useful and needed."
Immobilization	4	4–16	"Have there ever been times when you couldn't take care of things because you just couldn't get going?"
Perceived control	1	1–2	"Some people feel they can run their lives much the way they want to, others feel the problems of life are sometimes too big for them. Which one are you most like?"

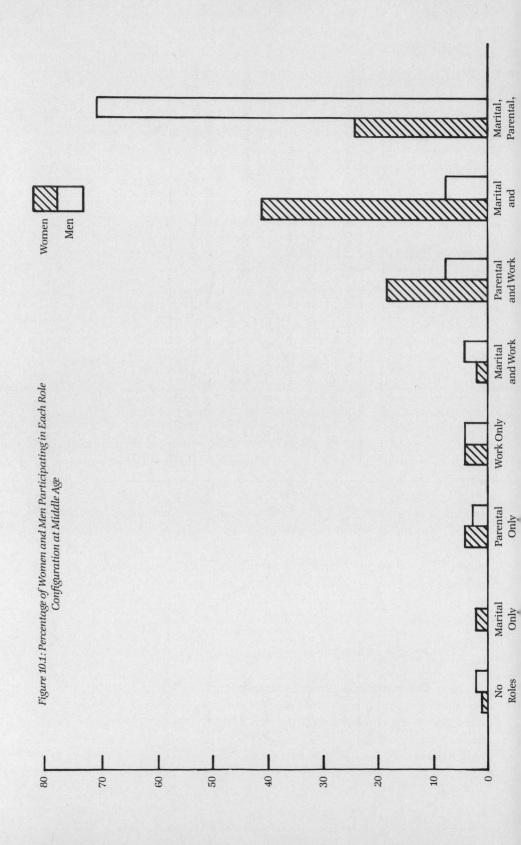

Figure 10.1: Percentage of Women and Men Participating in Each Role Configuration at Middle Age

in the work role only at midlife. Overall, people in single roles constituted a very small segment of our midlife sample.

Larger numbers of people were participating in dual roles. Some role constellations had larger proportions of people than others and we began also to see gender differences. A small portion of our sample participated in only the marital and work roles (2% of the women and 4% of the men). This group was comprised of married working people who did not have children. A much larger proportion of the sample is comprised of single, working parents. Twice as many women (18%) than men (8%) were single working parents. The next category, marital plus parental roles, demonstrated the traditional pattern of role configuration for women and men. Nearly six times as many women (41%) as men (8%) were in the marital and parental roles (homemaking role).

A major gender difference was also exhibited in the number of roles occupied. Nearly three-quarters of the men (71%) had three roles as opposed to one-quarter of the women (24%). In summary, most women and men at midlife were involved in multiple roles. The women in our sample were primarily homemakers, with a considerable percentage of single, working mothers and married, working mothers. In contrast, most of the men held the three roles simultaneously. Very few men were single parents, unemployed, or participating in a homemaker role.

One thing is clear from our figures: women's entrance into the paid labor market does not mean an automatic increase in the number of women occupying three roles. If women are marrying and having children later and divorcing more, then their participation in the paid labor market can sometimes mean a change in roles rather than an increase in the number of roles occupied. How is it that men managed to occupy three roles more frequently than did women? The answer lies no doubt in the fact that the domestic roles have traditionally, and do still, make far greater demands on female occupants than on male occupants. Whether or not they are in the paid labor force, women do the great majority of childcare and household labor (Aneshensel, Frerichs, and Clark, 1981; Crosby, 1982).

Predicting Well-being in Midlife

Given that the women and men in the sample differed in the constellation of roles they occupy, and presumably in the nature of those roles, what is the association between gender, roles, and well-being? To answer the question, we first performed a number of multiple regression analyses in which we examined the associations between each measure of health, on the one hand, and gender, role, and other demographic characteristics, on the other. Specifically, in the regressions we used role configurations as predictor variables while also controlling for other sociodemographic factors like education and income that might influence mental and physical health. Because of our interest in the effect of paid employment on well-being, we developed a series of variables comparing different role configurations involving work with all other role configurations which did not include employment as a role (that is, where 0 = role(s) not including paid employment, 1 = each of the following role configurations): employment only, employment and parenthood, employment and marriage, employment and parenthood and marriage. Analyses for men and women were conducted separately.

Physical health was clearly related to role configuration as well as family income for both men and women (table 10.2). The work role both singly and in combination with any other role or roles decreased the likelihood that one suffered from poor health. Men with dual and triple roles and men with the single role of employment enjoyed better health than men who were not employed. The effect was more selective for women. Women who were employed and parents and women who were employed wives and parents reported better health than nonemployed women. Ample family income also helped both men and women. Apparently, although employment appeared to have a positive effect on men regardless of other roles, this relationship was true only for women who combined paid employment in certain specified role configurations.

Examination of the relationship between role configuration and psychological anxiety indicated a somewhat different pattern (table 10.2). The analysis for men did not reach conventional levels of statistical significance, but the analysis for women once again indicated that employment is an important role. Employed married women and employed married mothers had significantly lower levels of psychological anxiety than women who were not employed. Neither family income nor education influenced this relationship.

The third regression analysis explored the relationship between self-esteem, the four role configuration variables outlined above, family income, and education (table 10.3). For men, only education was a significant predictor of self-esteem. For women, however, the dual role configuration of employment and parenthood as well as the triple role configuration of employment, marriage, and parenthood were both significant predictors of self-esteem. Women with both these role configurations had higher levels of self-esteem than women without employment in their role configurations.

Employment appeared to be a very important determinant of depression

Table 10.2: Regression Analyses of Health, Psychological Anxiety, and Self-esteem

	Health		Psychological anxiety		Self-esteem	
	b	beta	b	beta	b	beta
Men						
Employment only	2.66	.18**	.26	.03	.58	.06
Employment + parenthood	3.51	.29***	−.71	−.08	.90	.12
Employment + marriage	3.96	.25***	.23	.02	.89	.09
Employment, parenthood, marriage	2.99	.42***	−.06	−.01	.64	.14
Family income	.18	.22**	−.04	−.08	.07	.13
Education	.06	.06	−.02	−.02	.10	.15*
F	13.48***		.73		4.52***	
R^2	.231		.016		.091	
Adj. R^2	.214		.000		.071	
Women						
Employment only	1.63	.09	−.83	−.07	.11	.01
Employment + parenthood	1.94	.20**	−.44	−.07	.67	.14*
Employment + marriage	1.36	.06	−1.82	−.11*	.69	.06
Employment, parenthood, marriage	1.39	.17**	−1.00	−.18**	.81	.19**
Family income	.21	.27***	−.04	−.07	.05	.12
Education	.15	.12	−.06	−.07	.06	.09
F	11.48***		3.79***		5.21***	
R^2	.166		.062		.083	
Adj. R^2	.152		.046		.067	

*$p < .05$ **$p < .01$ ***$p < .001$

Table 10.3: Regression Analyses of Depression, Immobilization and Perceived Control

	Depression		Immobilization		Perceived control	
Men	b	beta	b	beta	b	beta
Employment only	−1.27	−.06	−.69	−.08	−.10	−.07
Employment + parenthood	−3.73	−.22**	−.77	−.12	−.05	−.04
Employment + marriage	−4.58	−.21**	−1.73	−.20**	.12	.08
Employment, parenthood, marriage	−2.94	−.30***	−1.03	−.27**	.02	.03
Family income	−.13	−.12	.03	.08	.02	.22**
Education	.02	.01	.01	.02	.00	.01
F	4.66***		1.76***		3.73***	
R^2	.094		.038		.078	
Adj. R^2	.074		.016		.057	
Women						
Employment only	2.04	.08	.53	.05	.01	.01
Employment + parenthood	−.13	−.01	−.27	−.05	−.02	−.02
Employment + marriage	−3.16	−.09	−.60	−.04	.02	.01
Employment, parenthood, marriage	−1.17	−.10	−.83	−.18**	−.02	−.02
Family income	−.13	−.12	.01	.02	.01	.06
Education	−.19	−.11	−.07	−.09	.03	.18**
F	5.16***		2.84*		2.79*	
R^2	.082		.047		.048	
Adj. R^2	.067		.030		.031	

*p < .05   **p < .01   ***p < .001

for men (Crosby, 1982; Gove and Geerken, 1977; Radloff, 1975; Weissman and Klerman, 1977). Men who were employed parents, men who were employed husbands, and men who were employed married fathers were all significantly less likely to report being depressed than other men. This relationship did not hold for men who were employed only (neither married nor parents), and these relationships were not affected by family income or education. It is interesting that the analyses for women indicated that role configuration is not significantly predictive of depression, although the pattern of results suggested that employment plus marriage, and employment plus marriage and parenthood safeguard women from depression. Similarly, there was a tendency for wealthier people to be less depressed, but this relationship also did not reach conventional levels of significance (table 10.3).

Immobilization was also significantly related to role configurations for both men and women. Men who were both employed and married and men who were employed married fathers were less likely to report immobilization. For women, only the triple role configuration—that is, being employed, married, and a parent—minimized immobilization. Women who occupied all three roles were less likely to report feeling immobilized (table 10.3).

Role configuration among men and women was not significantly related to perceptions of control (table 10.3). Men who reported higher family income were significantly more likely to report feelings of perceived control. Similarly, women with higher levels of education were more likely to report higher levels of perceived control.

These data clearly show that employment predicted well-being and health (table 10.4). This effect, although present for men, appeared to be much more prevalent for women. In addition, it is important to note that, while employment had salutary effects, the best mental and physical health occurred when it was complemented by other roles. In general, the triple role configuration of employment, marriage, and parenthood appeared to be the most consistently and positively related to health and well-being, especially for women.

Role Combinations and Well-being

Is work important in and of itself or does its impact on well-being depend on a person's entire configuration of roles? To look in greater depth at the association between our measures of physical and mental health, on the one hand, and gender and role configuration, on the other,

Table 10.4: *Significant Predictors of Well-being at Midlife*

	Men	*Women*
Physical health	employment employment + parenthood employment + marriage employment + parenthood 　　　　+ marriage family income	employment + parenthood employment + parenthood 　　　　+ marriage family income
Psychological anxiety	none	employment + marriage employment + parenthood 　　　　+ marriage
Self-esteem	family income education	employment + parenthood employment + parenthood 　　　　+ marriage
Depression	employment + parenthood employment + marriage employment + parenthood 　　　　+ marriage	none
Immobilization	employment + marriage employment + parenthood 　　　　+ marriage	employment + parenthood 　　　　+ marriage
Perceived control	family income	education

we partitioned the women and men into various role combinations. The distribution of scores among various groups confirmed the conclusion that well-being was closely associated, among our national probability sample, with participation in the paid labor market (tables 10.5 and 10.6).

Physical health differed by role configurations for both women and men. Women who were single nonworking parents were in the poorest health, while working women without children and the women involved in three roles were in better physical health. Similarly, the men in the nonworking parental role but who were also married reported the most health problems. Like the women, men involved in marital and work roles (without the parental role) were in the best health.

Psychological anxiety also varied by role configuration (table 10.5). Single nonworking mothers had the most anxiety and the married working women without children had the least. Men's anxiety was not related to role configuration.

Mean levels of self-esteem varied substantially by role configuration (table 10.5). Women who were married and employed and women participating in all three roles had the highest self-esteem, while nonworking

Table 10.5: Physical Health, Psychological Anxiety, and Self-Esteem by Role Configuration

	Physical Health			Psychological Anxiety			Self-Esteem		
	N	Mean	Standard Deviation	N	Mean	Standard Deviation	N	Mean	Standard Deviation
Men									
No Roles	6	18.50	2.95	6	9.00	3.29	5	14.00	1.40
Marital only	—	—	—	—	—	—	—	—	—
Parental only	5	18.80	3.84	5	7.40	2.69	6	12.50	2.25
Work only	13	19.54	4.55	13	8.62	2.19	13	13.23	1.80
Marital and parental	22	15.45	1.57	23	8.61	1.73	23	12.13	3.24
Marital and work	12	21.50	4.60	12	8.42	2.59	13	13.62	1.40
Parental and work	22	20.68	2.44	22	7.55	1.92	22	13.77	1.77
Marital, parental, and work	208	20.70	2.53	208	8.15	2.18	208	13.67	1.89
Total and Overall Mean	288	20.20	3.14	280	8.18	2.23	290	13.52	2.02
Women									
No Roles	3	16.00	6.93	4	7.75	2.36	4	12.75	1.50
Marital only	7	16.29	4.39	7	10.29	2.63	7	12.57	2.70
Parental only	25	15.72	3.22	25	11.16	2.24	25	12.28	2.34
Work only	17	19.71	4.89	17	8.53	3.14	17	12.77	1.30
Marital and parental	161	19.10	3.37	161	9.27	2.33	160	12.97	1.88
Marital and work	8	20.75	3.36	8	7.50	2.35	8	13.75	1.39
Parental and work	70	19.94	3.35	70	9.29	2.46	70	13.40	1.73
Marital, parental, and work	95	20.40	2.67	94	8.39	2.11	95	13.72	1.46
Total and Overall Mean	386	19.34	3.56	386	9.11	2.46	386	13.18	1.81

unmarried mothers and nonworking married women without children had the lowest self-esteem. These findings suggest that participation in the work role may have an important impact on the self-esteem of women. Among the men, there were also differences with regard to role configuration. Men with no roles and those participating in dual or multiple roles (parental and work, marital and work, and marital, parental, and work) which included employment had the highest self-esteem. It should be noted that there were only six men in the no-roles category. Among men without the work role, nonworking men who were married and parents had the lowest self-esteem.

The findings for role configuration and depression were similar (table 10.6). Work figured importantly in how depressed a person felt at midlife. The most depressed among the women were nonworking single mothers and the least depressed were women involved in the work and marital role. Similar to the depressed nonworking women, the men who were not working and had children (men participating in the marital and parental roles) were the most depressed. Among the least depressed were men who participated in the marital and work roles, the parental and work roles, and no roles.

The different role configurations were associated with differing levels of immobilization (table 10.6). Women who were married but neither parents nor working reported the highest levels of immobilization, while women who had no roles or all three roles reported the least amount of immobilization. While it is not clear why women with no roles reported the least amount of immobilization, it should be noted that there were only four people in this category. The mean levels of immobilization did not vary to a great extent with the role configurations for men.

On the final measure, perceived control, the scores of women did not differ with respect to social roles, but men's scores did. Inspection of the means in table 10.6 shows that most women reported having similar amounts of control. Among the men, however, those who had no roles or who were in the marital and work roles reported having more control of their lives. Interestingly, the men who were single unemployed parents reported having the least amount of control in their lives.

In summary, it appears that the social roles that women and men occupied were linked to their psychological and physical well-being at midlife. The work role, in particular, was important to well-being across most of the measures and may have been especially crucial in situations where there was no spouse or no other sources of income.

Table 10.6: *Depression, Immobilization, and Perceived Control by Role Configuration*

	Depression			Immobilization			Perceived control		
	N	Mean	Standard Deviation	N	Mean	Standard Deviation	N	Mean	Standard Deviation
Men									
No Roles	5	10.60	3.40	6	6.67	1.75	6	2.00	.00
Marital only	—	—	—	—	—	—	—	—	—
Parental only	6	14.33	5.70	5	7.80	1.82	6	1.67	.45
Work only	13	13.31	6.50	13	6.85	3.19	12	1.75	.51
Marital and parental	22	15.68	5.50	22	7.64	.79	23	1.83	.00
Marital and work	13	10.39	3.45	12	5.92	1.84	13	2.00	.38
Parental and work	22	10.59	3.20	22	6.64	2.08	23	1.83	.38
Marital, parental, and work	208	11.15	4.00	207	6.62	1.66	200	1.93	.25
Total Overall Mean	289	11.57		287	13.52	1.74	213	1.91	.29
Women									
No Roles	4	13.25	5.31	4	5.25	1.5	4	1.50	.58
Marital only	7	14.71	8.67	7	8.14	2.79	6	1.67	.52
Parental only	25	15.36	6.63	25	7.48	2.09	24	1.67	.40
Work only	17	15.06	6.27	17	7.59	2.18	16	1.81	.48
Marital and parental	160	12.64	4.86	161	7.04	1.51	152	1.80	.35
Marital and work	8	9.25	3.28	8	6.50	2.01	8	1.88	.40
Parental and work	71	13.58	4.98	69	6.91	2.10	68	1.77	.43
Marital, parental, and work	95	11.53	4.16	95	6.33	1.68	93	1.81	.40
Total and Overall Mean	387	12.80	5.09	386	6.88	2.00	371	1.78	.41

Multiple roles at midlife provide benefits for both women and men, and the work role appears to be particularly vital for mental and physical health. Not working for pay outside of the home appears to be stressful for both women and men, although nonworking women (the majority of whom list themselves as homemakers) have some social status and financial security (realized through their husbands) that nonworking or unemployed men do not. Clearly, many married women with employed husbands have the option of not working without suffering any serious social stigmatization, but, in this culture, working is not only linked to a person's identity and primary role (as breadwinner) but the lack of employment appears to have serious negative implications for all other aspects of life. Nonworking men often describe themselves as agitated, upset, guilty, ashamed, and bored (Kahn, 1981). In this study they, along with nonworking single mothers, were in poor mental and physical health. Thus, we may find in future research that homemakers are in better physical and psychological shape than unemployed men, but unemployed female heads of households may feel as demoralized as unemployed men. Such changes may already have begun in the ten years since these data were collected.

One could argue that multiple roles have an important function at any point in the life-cycle. Work is often prominent in the initiation and termination of many major life-cycle periods (for example, young adulthood, midlife, retirement). Recently, however, midlife has come to be seen as a special period in which the self is highlighted and both women and men use their social roles as a yardstick for measuring their accomplishments thus far and the probability of achieving their life goals in the time remaining. Future studies can provide a detailed analysis of how the personal and situational factors characterizing multiple roles influence the subjective and objective experience of midlife. In addition, research on black women and men and other groups with differing cultural expectations and values regarding the integration of work and family life will also increase our understanding of the importance of multiple roles in adult development. We also need more studies examining the reciprocal relation between multiple roles and well-being. Physical health, particularly at middle age and older ages, may be as instrumental as multiple roles in the psychological well-being of women and men. Finally, longitudinal studies which investigate multiple roles at a variety of life-cycle stages (young adult, middle age, retirement age) will further explicate the function of roles for women and men.

This chapter suggests that previous research on well-being which uses gender as a major explanatory variable and links gender differences to psychological and physical health may be less informative than research focusing on paid employment and role configurations. Historically, society has prescribed two roles for women: the marital and parental roles. The greater depression, psychological anxiety, and lower self-esteem of women which has been attributed to biological differences by some may be better accounted for by patterns of role occupancy. It is evident from our research and from a growing number of studies that work in combination with parenting and marriage plays a dominant part in the well-being of middle-aged adults. Work and family add meaning to adulthood and help promote physical and psychological well-being.

References

Aneshensel, C. S., Frerichs, R. R., and Clark, V. A. (1981). Family roles and sex differences in depression. *Journal of Health and Social Behavior*, 22, 379–93.

Chesler, P. (1972). *Women and madness*. New York: Avon Books.

Cleary, P. D., and Mechanic, D. (1983). Sex differences in psychological distress among married people. *Journal of Health and Social Behavior*, 24, 111–21.

Crosby, F. (1982). *Relative deprivation and working women*. New York: Oxford University Press.

Gove, W. R., and Geerken, M. R. (1977). The effect of children and employment on the mental health of married men and women. *Social Forces*, 56, 66–76.

Kahn, R. L. (1981). *Work and health*. New York: Wiley and Sons.

Kish, L., and Hess, I. (1965). *The Survey Research Center's national sample of dwellings*. Ann Arbor, Mich.: Institute for Social Research.

Pearlin, L. I. (1975). Sex roles and depression. In N. Datan and L. Ginsberg (eds.), *Proceedings of Fourth Life-Span Developmental Psychology Conference: Normative Life Crises*. New York: Academic Press.

Radloff, L. (1975). Sex differences in depression: The effects of occupation and marital status. *Sex Roles*, 1, 249–60.

Rosenberg, M. (1965). *Society and the adolescent self-image*. Princeton: Princeton University Press.

Verbrugge, L. M. (1983). Multiple roles and physical health of women and men. *Journal of Health and Social Behavior*, 24, 16–30.

Veroff, J., Douvan, E., and Kulka, R. (1981). *The inner American*. New York: Basic Books.

Weissman, M. M., and Klerman, G. L. (1977). Sex differences and the epidemiology of depression. *Archives of General Psychiatry*, 34, 98–111.

Zung, W. W. (1965). A self-rating depression scale. *Archives of General Psychology*, 12, 63–70.

11

Role Responsibilities, Role Burdens, and Physical Health

Lois M. Verbrugge

Adult roles contain obligations and burdens as well as pleasures, and each role a person has can be experienced as more or less burdensome. What is the relationship between role burdens and physical health among men and women? The answers come from a survey conducted in 1978 assessing role responsibilities, role burdens, and physical health among a sample of over 700 adults living in the Detroit metropolitan area.

Previous research has concentrated on how role *occupancy* (simply having a particular role) relates to health. A number of studies have firmly documented the relationship between paid employment and good physical health. Also well established are the links between good health and marriage and, somewhat more tenuously, between good health and parenthood. In general, the more life roles one occupies, the better one's health is (Verbrugge, 1986). Researchers have typically paid less attention to the *quality* of one's life roles, but a few observations seem well supported. Dissatisfaction with important life roles is associated with poor health (Hauenstein, Kasl, and Harburg, 1977; Verbrugge, 1982). Poor social support at work, and especially poor interactions with one's boss, undermine health (Haynes and Feinleib, 1980; Hibbard and Pope, 1985).

With past research as a guide, I shall examine here data from the Health In Detroit study (Verbrugge, 1979, 1980, 1984). A multi-stage probability sample of white households in the Detroit metropolitan area was selected in fall, 1978. In each household, one adult was chosen as the study respondent by a random procedure, and an initial interview was conducted at the home. Following the interview, respondents kept daily health records for six weeks about physical symptoms and actions taken for them. Altogether

714 people (412 women, 302 men) were interviewed, and 589 of them (346 women, 243 men) kept at least one week of daily health records. At the end of the project, a termination interview was conducted by telephone.

Physical Health of Women and Men

I will study physical health with measures from both the initial interview and the daily health records. Table 11.1 presents the measures and shows that, on all of them, women reported poorer health than men.

Table 11.1: *Gender and Physical Health*

	Health Variables	*Mean Scores among:* *Men*	*Women*	*Statistical Significance of Sex Difference*
Initial Interview	Self-rated health status (1 = excellent; 5 = poor)	1.86	2.10	NS
	Number of chronic conditions and symptoms in last year	3.69	4.52	$p < .01$
	Number of days of restricted activity due to illness/injury in past year	17.4	20.2	NS
	Job limitations due to health (1 = none; 2 = limited in kind of job/amount of work; 3 = unable to hold job)	1.28	1.33	NS
	Number of medications used for chronic problems	1.00	1.74	$p < .01$
Daily Health Records	Daily feelings of health (average over 6 weeks) (1 = wonderful; 10 = terrible)	2.74	3.02	$p < .05$
	Number of health problems experienced in six weeks	17.1	27.1	$p < .01$
	Number of days of restricted activity in six weeks	3.3	4.6	$p < .05$
	Number of prescription drugs taken in six weeks	17.3	26.0	$p < .05$

Note: NS = not significant

The gender differences were statistically significant for two of the five interview items and for all four of the daily record items.

Why were the women in poorer health? Could it be explained by demographic, social, or psychological factors that affect health and, at the same time, differ for men and women? Women in the survey tended to exceed men on several key characteristics that predict poor health: they were slightly older than the men; they were less likely to be employed for pay; and, when employed, they were likely to have lower-status jobs. I conducted a series of statistical tests taking into account these age, employment status, and occupational level differences. The tests answer the question, "How would men's and women's health differ if the sexes were the same in these three characteristics?" The gender differences in health narrowed greatly. In fact, in a few items there were reversals—more health troubles among men than women. Men had more restricted activity (during the past year and also during the six weeks of reporting) and more job limitations.

Role Responsibilities, Role Burdens, and Health

The importance of employment status in the relationship between gender and health suggests that physical health might be closely linked to role responsibilities and burdens. Are heavy role responsibilities and burdens associated with poor health? Are those relationships the same for women and men? For each participant in the study, I assessed role responsibilities and burdens in a number of ways. All of the measures depended on self-report. Some—such as the number of life roles occupied and the number of hours worked—were more objective, and some, such as feelings of time pressure, were more subjective in nature. For the purposes at hand, I call the more objective aspects "role responsibilities" and the more subjective ones "role burdens."

Role Responsibilities

I grouped role responsibilities into three types: role involvement, time constraints, and family responsibilities (table 11.2). *Role involvement* was measured first by the number of main life roles a person occupied: worker, spouse, parent. Next, the number of activities was based on the three main life roles, volunteer work, and any other regularly scheduled activity. Income fraction was calculated by determining the percentage of household income the respondent produced. Income burden was a more complex variable derived by multiplying income fraction by the number of people in the household. *Time constraint* variables included the hours per week

Table 11.2: *Health as a Function of Role Responsibilities*

| | Health | | | | | | | | |
| | Initial Interview | | | | | Daily Health Records | | | |
Role Responsibilities	Health status	Chronic conditions	Restricted activity days in year	Job limitations	Current medications for chronic problems	Daily physical feelings	Health problems in six weeks	Restricted activity days in six weeks	Prescription drugs in six weeks
A. Role Involvements									
1. Number of roles	+	+					+	+	
2. Number of activities	+	+	+				+	+	
3. Income fraction						+		+	
4. Income burden								+	
B. Time Constraints and Schedules									
1. Hours constrained per week			+				+		
2. Length of work day									
3. Regular work week									
4. Total work days per week									
C. Family Responsibilities									
·1. Number of children									
2. Number of preschool children									
3. Index of total dependency									

Note: A plus sign indicates that the role responsibility predicted levels on the health item over and above effects of age, occupational status, and other control variables.

constrained by fixed activities, the length of the work day, whether the respondent worked a regular work week, and number of days worked per week. (The last three were recorded for employed people only). Finally, measures of *family responsibilities* were based on dependents at home: the number of the respondent's children there, the number of preschool children in the household, and an index of total dependency, based on a weighted average of elderly people and children of different ages.

I performed a set of multiple regression analyses to discover how these variables related to the nine measures of health among the women and men in the sample (table 11.2).[1] When a plus (+) appears in a column, it means that the role responsibility predicted levels on the health item, over and above any effects of age, occupational status, and other control variables.

It is readily apparent that certain role involvements affect health. The more roles people occupy, the better their health. People who occupied none of the three major roles had extremely poor health. The same applied to activities: the more, the better, and those individuals with no regular activities suffered many more health problems than others. The link between high role involvement and good health comes, no doubt, from two processes: social selection and social causation. People with long-term health problems probably restrict the activities in their lives and are unable to maintain numerous life roles. This is social selection. Social causation probably also operated in the Detroit study. Roles give people the opportunity to express their diverse skills and also to gain access to social supports, resources, and social stimulation (Thoits, 1983), and these can act to help maintain physical and mental health.

More complex than the relationships between health and the numbers of roles and activities were the relationships between health and financial

1. Multiple Classification Analysis (MCA) was used to estimate the effects of predictors and controls on health (Andrews et al., 1973). For MCA, all independent variables must be categorical and the dependent variable must be interval-scaled. I condensed the original scores of independent variables into categories when necessary. All dependent variables were interval to start with.

For each role burden predictor, three models were estimated:

0. $\hat{Y} = f$ [Age, Other controls] Control model
1. $\hat{Y} = f$ [Age, Other controls, Sex, Role responsibility/burden] Main effects model
2. $\hat{Y} = f$ [Age, Other controls, Sex times Role responsibility/burden] Interaction model.

For model 2, Sex times Role Responsibility/Burden is one variable which crosses the two sex categories with the n role item categories. It encompasses main plus interaction effects of the predictors. If the R^2 increment from model 1 to 2 is significant, this would signal that role burden effects differ for women and men. The three models were repeated for all nine health indexes.

There are four control variables in the analysis. Respondent's age appears in all models. In models that predict health behavior (medications, restricted days), I included a control for health status. The specific item varies (for initial interview items, it is the number of chronic problems in the past year; for restricted activity in six weeks, the number of symptomatic days in that period; for drugs in six weeks, the number of health problems in that period). In models with time constraint and family responsibility predictors, I controlled for employment status (currently employed, nonemployed). In models with job schedule predictors, I also included occupational status (upper white collar, lower white collar, upper blue collar, lower blue collar).

responsibility. Health did not vary by the income burden people experienced. Income fraction was slightly related to health in a curvilinear way: people who earned either very little or all of the income in a household had poorer health. More specifically, women and men who earned either less than 20 percent or 100 percent of the income in a household had more health problems than others. Again, both social selection and social causation offer plausible explanations of the observed relationships. People who were in very poor health were probably unable to produce much of the household income, while those who produced all the income in their households might have been stressed in so doing.

Making money takes time. It comes as no surprise, then, to find that the relationship between time constraints and physical health was also curvilinear. The Detroit women and men who had very few (less than twenty-five) or very many (seventy or more) hours per week of constrained time had poorer health than those in the middle. Social selection and social causation seem, once again, to be important in accounting for the relationships.

Family responsibilities had surprisingly small links to women's and men's health. But the effects looked curvilinear; that is, people with lowest and highest responsibility for dependents had worse health than people with moderate responsibility. If the study had more specific items about the actual time and duties involved in caring for dependents, I might have found stronger relationships to health. Research to date suggests that parenthood per se poses no problem for health but that high parenting demands may.

Role Burdens

Subjective reality does not correspond perfectly with objective reality. How burdened people *feel* with their life roles depends on many factors and is not determined simply by the roles themselves. While having numerous role responsibilities did not lead to ill health for Detroit people, it was conceivable that heavy role burdens did. By role burdens, I mean the subjective experience of life roles.

Measures of role burden are shown in table 11.3. Four items concern people's *feelings about their life and roles*. All of the respondents were asked to "think about your life during the past year" and to rank it on a ten-point scale where 1 meant "the worst life you could expect" and 10 "the best life you could expect." Next, all women in the survey (employed or not) and all the employed men were asked to evaluate their main life role. (Em-

Table 11.3: *Health as a Function of Role Burdens*

| | Health | | | | | Daily Health Records | | | |
| | Initial Interview | | | | | | | | |
Role Burdens	Health status	Chronic conditions	Restricted activity days in year	Job limitations	Current medications for chronic problems	Daily physical feelings	Health problems in six weeks	Restricted activity days in six weeks	Prescription drugs in six weeks
A. Feelings about life and roles									
1. Assessment of life in last year	+	+	+	+			+	+	
2. Feelings about main role								+	
3. Feelings about job (among employed people)		+					+	+	
4. Feelings about job and housework (among employed women)									
B. Time pressures									
1. Feel rushed		+				+			
2. Time on hands									
3. Over– and underinvolved		+		+					
4. Worn out at end of day	+	+	+			+	+	+	

Note: A plus sign indicates that the role burden predicted levels on the health item over and above effects of age, occupational status, and other control variables.

ployed women were asked whether paid employment or housework constituted their main life role.) Also, employed respondents answered an open-ended question about their jobs, phrased: "People feel differently about their jobs. Some look on their jobs as just something they have to do.

Others really enjoy their jobs. How about you? Apart from the money, how do you feel about your job?" The answers were coded into five categories. Finally, a combined score was computed for the employed women to indicate how positively they felt about both their job and their housework.

The other measures relate to *time pressures*. Respondents were asked how much of the time they felt rushed, how often they had idle time, if they felt involved in too many activities, and how often they felt "worn out" when done with their work or household tasks.

How people felt about their lives and their life roles proved extremely important in predicting their health. All of the effects shown in table 11.3 were strong and monotonic (not curvilinear). The more people disliked their lives, their main roles, or their jobs, the worse was their health. As general contentment with life declined, health dropped sharply. Concerning job satisfaction, people who stated negative feelings about their jobs tended to have distinctly worse health than other workers. The health of employed women did not generally vary by the combined measure of job and housework satisfaction, with one important exception: women who disliked *both* their employment and their housework roles did have extremely poor health.

Subjective time pressures also proved important for health among the Detroit adults. Here, some curvilinear patterns appeared. People who always felt rushed or never felt rushed were in worse health than people with more moderate experiences. The same held true for feeling over- or underinvolved. Women and men who reported that they felt very overinvolved or very underinvolved also reported more symptoms and more job limitations due to ill health than did other people. The other two items show simpler patterns: as idle time increases or people feel worn out often, health worsens. These items are probably consequences of poor health, instead of causes. That is, people in very poor health reduce their activities and become tired readily.

Comparisons

A comparison of tables 11.2 and 11.3 shows clearly that role burdens mattered much more than role responsibilities for the health of people in the Health In Detroit study. How a person felt about his or her life roles generally predicted health quite well, over and above the effects from control variables including age. Generally, the more burdened people felt, the worse was their health. This did not mean, however, that health deteriorated as objective role responsibilities increased. On the contrary, the people with three major life roles (worker, spouse, parent) exhibited the best health by far, followed by the people with two major life roles, then one, and finally, far below, people with none.

How important were role burdens and role responsibilities compared to age, occupational level, or other control variables? To determine the relative importance of factors, I divided the health items into those relating to health status (such as the number of chronic problems) and those relating to health behavior (such as taking medications, restricting activity). I then determined how much of the variation in health status was due to demographic factors like age, versus the measures of role responsibility and role burden.[2] I looked finally at the health behaviors as a function of demographic factors, role responsibilities/burdens, and also health status.

The statistical analyses for health status revealed that the strongest associations were with age. As people advanced in age, their health declined. Employment status ranked second, with paid employment linked to good health. Role responsibilities and burdens came next. For health behavior, the most important predictor was, understandably, health status. It was followed by employment status and, to a much smaller degree, age. Role responsibilities and role burdens typically ranked just after age as important predictors of health behavior. Much less important than any of the other variables as a predictor of health status and of health behaviors was gender. As I noted earlier, the initial gender differences are largely explained by the simple facts that the Detroit women and men differed in age, employment status, and occupations.

In further analyses, I asked if role responsibilities and burdens influence men's and women's health similarly, or if one sex reacts more strongly to them.[3] The answer is clear in the Detroit study. The monotonic connections between the number of roles/activities on the one hand and good health on the other operated in the same way for women as for men. So did the curvilinear relationships between financial responsibilities and health, between time constraints and health, and between subjective role burdens and health. In sum, the numerous connections between role responsibilities/burdens and health operated in the same ways for women and men.

2. To assess strength of effects I looked at beta coefficients of the MCA's for model 1.
3. I assess these special effects by comparing model 2 (Interaction) with model 1 (Main effects). Of the 171 tests for the R^2 increment from model 1 to 2, none is statistically significant. The increments are numerically very small, ranging from .000 to .031.

Gender, Role Responsibilities, and Role Burdens

To say that role responsibilities and role burdens predicted health status and health behavior in the same way for women and men is not to say that women and men experienced the same *degree* of role responsibility and role burden in their lives. Table 11.4 displays the degree to which the women and men in the study differed in their role responsibilities. Men had greater role involvements and greater objective time constraints. Men and women had the same family responsibilities, in the sense that they had the same numbers of dependents in their families. (Other measures of family responsibility, such as who is in charge of housework and childcare, would show differences.)

Table 11.5 shows gender differences in role burdens, the subjective experiences that may accompany role responsibilities. Women and men differed slightly in their feelings about roles and much more in their overall evaluations of life during the previous year. Men viewed their lives in the past year as generally good, eschewing very negative or very positive evaluations. By contrast, more women viewed their lives as either terrible or wonderful. Feelings of time pressure were very similar for the sexes. Women and men felt comparably rushed, devoid of idle time, and worn out at the end of the day. Men were slightly more likely to feel involved in too many activities, while women more often felt their number of activities was just right.

Several rather broad conclusions emerge from the Health In Detroit study. First, it is the perceived low quality of roles, not their high quantity, that puts people at risk for poor health. The benefits from role accumulation clearly outweigh the costs of increased stress. Second, as a consequence of both fewer roles and less positive feelings about their lives, women suffer poorer health than men. Third, the health outcome of a particular role responsibility or burden (say, always feeling rushed) is the same for the men and women who experience it.

Some knotty problems remain for scientists. First, is there an upper limit to the number of key roles that a person can occupy and still enjoy good health? I focused on three key roles. What if the array were larger? Second, how can one disentangle social selection and social causation? How, in other words, can the researcher know whether ill health is causing role limitations versus when absense of roles causes ill health? Longitudinal studies would obviously enhance our ability to map causal relationships.

Table 11.4: *Role Responsibilities of Men and Women*

	Percentages		Statistical Significance
	Men	*Women*	
A. Role Involvements			
1. Number of roles			
0	4.6%	13.4%	
1	30.1	35.4	
2	25.2	35.1	p < .01
3	40.1	16.1	
2. Number of activities			
0	2.0%	5.6%	
5	6.0	2.9	p < .01
3. Income fraction			
under 20%	4.0%	33.4%	
100%	60.6	24.6	p < .01
4. Income burden			
high	49.4%	9.4%	p < .01
B. Time Constraints			
1. Number of constrained hours per week			
0 – 24	8.9%	18.7%	
25 – 59	37.4	54.6	p < .01
60 – 69	25.8	15.3	
70 plus	28.9	21.4	
2. Length of work day			
long day (10–17 hrs)	26.6%	12.0%	p < .01
3. Regular work week			
No	10.2%	18.7%	p < .01
4. Total work days per week			
6 or 7 days	29.5%	13.5%	p < .01
C. Family Responsibilities			
1. Respondent's children in the household			
0	49.6%	52.0%	
3 or more	13.9	14.9	NS
2. Respondent's preschool children in the household			
2 or more	14.2%	11.1%	NS
3. Index of total dependency (children and elderly)			
No dependents	46.6%	46.3%	
High dependency	8.0	5.8	NS

Note: NS = not significant.

Table 11.5: *Role Burdens of Men and Women*

	Percentages		Statistical Significance
	Men	Women	
A. Feeling about Life and Roles			
1. Assessment of life in past year			
bad (score 1–4)	4.7%	9.0%	
good (7–8)	46.7	37.0	p < .01
excellent (10)	12.0	18.8	
2. Feelings about main role			
unqualified liking	59.0%	53.7%	
qualified liking	8.6	9.8	NS
mixed	25.4	30.1	
dislike	7.0	6.4	
3. Feelings about job (among employed people)			
unqualified liking	59.0%	67.6%	
qualified liking	8.6	5.7	NS
mixed	25.4	20.0	
dislike	7.0	6.9	
4. Feelings about job and housework (among employed women)			
definitely like both	—	27.9%	—
mostly like both	—	13.0	
definitely dislike both	—	4.3	
B. Time Pressures			
1. Feel rushed			
always	8.6%	9.5%	
often	25.6	20.7	NS
never	8.6	7.6	
2. Time on hands			
always or often	7.6%	6.3%	NS
3. Over- and under-involved			
too many things to do	15.7%	8.8%	
just right	50.6	55.7	p < .05
would like more	33.7	35.5	
4. Worn out at end of day			
every day	5.0%	7.8%	NS
often	14.3	17.8	

Note: NS = not significant

Social issues also emerge. How can women become more satisfied about their activities? And how can women increase their formal activities and commitments while avoiding extremely high time pressures? How can men diminish their difficulties with highly constrained hours and feelings of overcommitment? Not all of these changes are up to individuals themselves as they strive for a good life, including good health. Employers and spouses are important partners in helping workers, wives, and husbands achieve the middle ground of role obligations.

References

Andrews, F. M., Morgan, J. N., Sonquist, J. A., and Klem, L. (1973). *Multiple classification analysis*, 2d ed. Ann Arbor: Institute for Social Research, University of Michigan.

Hauenstein, L. S., Kasl, S. V., and Harburg, E. (1977). Work status, work satisfaction, and blood pressure among married black and white women. *Psychology of Women Quarterly*, 1, 334–39.

Haynes, S. G., and Feinleib, M. (1980). Women, work and coronary heart disease: Prospective findings from the Framingham Heart Study. *American Journal of Public Health*, 70, 133–41.

Hibbard, J. H., and Pope, C. R. (1985). Employment status, employment characteristics, and women's health. *Women and Health*, 10, 59–77.

Thoits, P. A. (1983). Multiple identities and psychological well-being: A reformulation and test of the social isolation hypothesis. *American Sociological Review*, 48, 174–87.

Verbrugge, L. M. (1979). Female illness rates and illness behavior: Testing hypotheses about sex differences in health. *Women and Health*, 4, 61–79.

———. (1980). Health diaries. *Medical Care*, 18, 73–95.

———. (1982). Work satisfaction and physical health. *Journal of Community Health*, 7, 262–83.

———. (1984). Health diaries: Problems and solutions in study design. In C. F. Cannell and R. M. Groves (eds.), *Health survey research methods*, pp. 171–92. Research Proceedings Series. DHHS Publ. No. PHS 84-3346, Rockville, Md.: National Center for Health Services Research.

———. (1986). Role burdens and physical health of women and men. *Women and Health*, 11, 47–77.

12

The Political Implications of Women's Statuses

Patricia Gurin

Most research that has documented the positive nature of a multiple-status lifestyle has emphasized its effects on life satisfaction and mental health, not on political beliefs and behavior. This book further details the personal consequences of multiple statuses, especially the circumstances under which they enhance rather than threaten well-being.

In this chapter, I consider the political impact of multiple statuses, specifically on women's gender consciousness and their participation in electoral politics. A multi-dimensional concept drawn from relative deprivation and solidarity/resource-mobilization theories, gender consciousness refers to the feelings and thoughts of women concerning the influence of gender on the lives and fortunes of men and women. The concept includes *identification*, the recognition of shared interests among women; *discontent*, the belief that women are deprived of power and influence relative to men; *withdrawal of legitimacy*, the belief that gender disparities in the marketplace are illegitimate, the result more of structural forces than of differences in the talents of men and women; and *collective orientation*, the belief that women should pool their resources to eliminate the obstacles that affect them as a group. *Electoral politics* includes voting and activities related to national and local election campaigns.

I analysed data collected from 1972 through 1983 by the Institute of Social Research at the University of Michigan to determine whether women who function in multiple statuses are more identified, discontented, critical of the legitimacy of gender-based stratification, and collectively oriented, and whether they vote and participate in election campaigns more

167

than women who perform in just a single status. Does a multiple-status lifestyle have these kinds of political consequences, as well as the more personal effects explored elsewhere in this volume?

To address this question, I first review the research literature on gender and politics, which attributes gender differences in voting and participation in electoral politics to traditional gender roles. We will see that employment and other experiences that have moved women out of their traditional statuses as homemakers and broadened their involvement in the public sphere have also fostered their gender consciousness and their participation in politics.

The importance of employment and homemaking raises a critical question. Is it a multiple-status lifestyle or a particular kind of status that theoretically promotes participation in politics and gender consciousness among women? The literature on women's multiple statuses is not very helpful in answering this question, since multiplicity is often confounded with a particular status. Most studies of the multiple statuses of women have explored the effects of adding the worker status to other statuses they already hold.

The relative importance of multiple and particular statuses is the central issue in this chapter. Drawing on Robert Merton's (1968) and Rose Coser's (1975) discussion of status-sets and role-sets, I suggest that the diversity, unfamiliarity, and instability of the role-sets associated with particular statuses are more important than their sheer number. After developing an argument as to why the properties of particular statuses should influence engagement in politics and evaluations of gender relations in society, I turn to analyses of survey data to assess the significance of multiplicity and particular statuses that take women out of the private sphere of home and family. I look at two in particular: entering the public world through employment and, for homemakers, participating in certain volunteer activities in the community.

Traditional Gender Roles: The Public and Private Spheres

Historically, men have voted in presidential and congressional elections at rates higher than women. Usually, the differential has been about 10 percent, although in 1980 women and men voted in equal numbers, and in 1984 turnout among women actually exceeded that of men (U. S. Bureau of the Census, 1985). More men than women have also participated in electoral campaigns and in other political activities, not only here but in Western Europe. Kent Jennings and Barbara Farah (1980) analyze data collected in 1974 in seven European nations and the United States on the participation of citizens in such activities as talking to others about politics, convincing others to vote for a certain candidate or party, attending a political meeting or rally, working for a political party or candidate, contacting a public official or politician, working with others to solve a local problem, and signing petitions. Comparing eight countries on these seven activities, they find not a single instance in which men do not exceed women in participation. Information collected in 1983 in the ten Common Market countries confirms that men still participate more than women in these kinds of political activity, although gender differences are smaller now than they were in the mid-1970s (Commission of the European Communities, 1984).[1]

Some scholars assert that the emphasis on campaign activities in these surveys has underestimated the political activity of women, which tends to focus on local issues and controversies that persist beyond election campaigns. In this regard, Virginia Sapiro (1984) stresses that much of what might be regarded as women's political work is considered social or personal because it does not take place under the institutional conditions usually associated with politics, nor does it receive the obvious reward of power; it is believed to be motivated by "nonpolitical" values of nurturance and social commitment. Although the various forms and targets of women's political action should certainly be documented, as should men's and women's interpretations of what is political, the question remains: why have women not participated as much as men in the conventional electoral and citizen acts that these surveys have traditionally measured?

The dominant model in political science explains the gender differences in two ways. First, socialization teaches young people not only that men and women generally assume different social roles but also that adult political expression is more of a male than a female activity (Jennings, 1983). Second, structural conditions give men and women unequal resources for participation in political life (Orum et al.,1974; Sapiro, 1983; Welch, 1980). The structural perspective stresses the pattern of social life that denies women the same opportunities and benefits accorded men (Krauss, 1974; Jennings, 1983). For example, women have only recently gained educational parity. Historically, educational inequality has been a

1. The gap in participation has always been smaller in the United States than in most countries in Western Europe (Barnes and Kasse, 1979; Jennings and Farah, 1980) and has decreased markedly since 1952, when the National Election Surveys at the University of Michigan first began monitoring the political behavior of the American electorate (Andersen, 1975; Baxter and Lansing, 1983; Christy, 1983; Welch, 1977).

critical political liability for women, since education has facilitated political activity in all the liberal democracies. Traditional gender roles further affect participation by enclosing women in the private sphere of the family and home while permitting, indeed demanding, the involvement of men in the public sphere.

The import of gender roles is the aspect of the structural argument that applies in particular to this book's focus on multiple statuses and roles. In political writing, the argument is made that the values characteristic of traditional roles for women in the private sphere are antithetical to the public sphere of politics. Entering politics as a candidate for office, as an activist in a political party, or as a campaign worker is thus not, for women who function exclusively as homemakers, a simple matter of taking up an additional activity. Rather, it means participating in activities and institutions populated primarily by men and based on the values of the public sphere. Politics is portrayed as a rough-and-tumble world, requiring competitiveness, comfort with power, even corruption, and the willingness to be assertive, if not aggressive (Sapiro, 1983). The political arena is alien in many ways to the demands, values, and relationships that prevail in the private sphere. In this way, the adult experience of the truly cloistered homemaker reinforces the values and expectations of childhood socialization that politics is a man's world.

According to the structural argument, the privatization of women in the homemaker status restricts resources that are considered helpful, if not necessary, for an active political life. Traditional gender roles presumably explain why women are less interested in politics than men, more reluctant to express political opinions in polls and surveys, consider themselves less knowledgeable about political matters (Commission of the European Communities, 1984; Christy, 1983; Sapiro, 1983), and feel less politically efficacious, that is, less sure that they can influence political leaders and events (Andersen, 1975). It is not only these psychological resources that are affected by gender roles. The homemaker status also limits organizational resources that are needed to participate in politics. Among them are opportunities to converse about politics and to gain access to political networks.

Employment and homemaking are the aspects of gender roles that have received the most attention. Only a few studies have examined the political impact of marriage and motherhood, as distinct from not working. The scanty evidence suggests that marriage has negligible influence on political participation (Sapiro, 1983; Welch, 1977) and does not depress political knowledge or other psychological resources that facilitate participation

(Sapiro, 1983). Motherhood—or more particularly, single motherhood—has proved somewhat negative, depressing both turnout and participation in campaign activities (Sapiro, 1983).

Most studies investigating the import of employment show that working in the paid labor force, although not nearly as important as education, has become increasingly influential since the early 1950s, particularly since the 1968 presidential election. Changes in employment patterns account in large part for the reduction in the gender gap in political participation over the past thirty years (Andersen, 1975; McDonagh, 1982; Welch, 1977). Since the late 1960s, there is evidence that the status of worker in the paid labor force has fostered registration and turnout (Welch, 1977), participation in campaign activities (Andersen, 1975; Christy, 1983; McDonagh, 1982), attendance at political meetings (Welch, 1977), attention to coverage of politics in the media, discussion of politics, and vote solicitation (Christy, 1983; Welch, 1977). Although some writers (Christy, 1983; Rossi, 1980) have warned of the contradictory potential of employment, increasing many resources but also decreasing the time available for political work, the research to date shows a positive influence even on the most time-consuming political activities (Christy, 1983; Welch, 1977).

There is some counterevidence reported in the research literature as well. From a longitudinal study of young women from age eighteen to twenty-six, Virginia Sapiro (1983) concludes that employment was not important either for participation or for the psychological resources that usually promote it. The only effect of employment was to increase the organizational resources of women, especially the number of communication networks in which they were embedded. However, since the women Sapiro studied were young adults, the effect of employment might have been weaker than is usually found in studies of national samples with a broad age range. The research literature on change in sex-role attitudes repeatedly shows that work is not a very powerful socializing experience for women in the years immediately after high school. Employment alters sex-role attitudes more, and thus might influence political outcomes more, when it occurs in the mature years (Ferree, 1981; Macke, Hudis, and Larrick, 1977) or after marriage (Thornton, Alwin, and Camburn, 1983). It has no effect on sex-role attitudes when it occurs right after high school (Spitze, 1978; Spitze and Waite, 1980) or prior to marriage (Thornton, Alwin, and Camburn, 1983). Employment thus seems more influential after the transition to adulthood, when women genuinely have assumed adult roles.

The positive impact of employment on support for more egalitarian gender roles among mature women suggests that the paid-worker status would also influence gender consciousness. The measures of sex-role attitudes used in the research literature on gender roles use normative statements about traditional roles. A woman is considered to believe that traditional sex-roles are illegitimate if she agrees that it is *appropriate* for a woman with preschool children to take a full-time job even if her husband doesn't particularly like it and that it's *perfectly all right* for women to be very active in clubs, politics, and other outside activities before her children are grown. If, on the other hand, a woman agrees that most of the important decisions in the life of the family *should* be made by the man of the house, that there is some work that is men's and some that is women's and they *should not* be doing each other's, that a wife *should not* expect her husband to help around the house after he comes home from work, and that it is much *better* for everyone if the man earns the main living and the woman takes care of the home and family, then the woman sees traditional sex roles as legitimate.

A direct test of the impact of gender roles on appraisals of legitimacy is reported by Crosby (1982). Crosby studied evaluations of women's employment given by a sample of married men and women, some homemakers and some working in the paid labor force. Gender role was far more important than gender in predicting responses. Homemakers and men expressed much the same views, while employed women were consistently the most critical of the gender stratification in the labor market. They were more resentful than homemakers about women's pay and fringe benefits, hours of work, chances for advancement, job challenge, respect on the job, job security, and general working conditions. They more often believed that the average working woman gets less than she wants or deserves from her job, and they were less optimistic that employed women would do well in the labor market in the next five or so years. There was only one way in which Crosby's homemakers were as critical of legitimacy as were her employed women: the two groups agreed that men are paid better than women. Employed men did not perceive the discrepancy as clearly.

I have also studied the specific tie between employment and gender consciousness. In a longitudinal national sample of women I was able to show the significance of employment in altering women's gender consciousness (Gurin, Thornton, and O'Brien, 1985). Analyzing individual change between 1972 and 1976 of women who were initially thirty years of age or older, I found that employment in the intervening years was an important influence on becoming more identified with other women, critical of legitimacy, and collectively discontented. I also examined other ways in which women sometimes enter the public sphere or shift out of aspects of the traditional homemaker status—for example, going back to school, leaving marriage, or attending religious services less often. Labor force experience proved more important than any other status change. It was work experience in particular that caused the broadest changes in gender consciousness.

In summary, the importance of homemaking and work-force statuses seems well established in these areas of research. Increases in the number of women who work outside the home and in their years of schooling have dramatically increased their political integration and brought about a new feminist consciousness. Apart from youth, schooling and employment most influence approval of egalitarianism in the household division of labor and criticism of gender differentiation and stratification in other social institutions.

Despite empirical support for the privatization thesis, it has been applied too simplistically at times and has been criticized for this reason by feminist scholars (Bourque and Grossholtz, 1974; Goot and Reid, 1975). The separation of the private and public spheres and the privatization of women's lives are often exaggerated. In fact, the image of women in the private, cloistered world of the home would no longer fit most women in the United States even if employment were used as the sole indicator of women's participation in the public sphere. More to the point, employment is *not* the only path from the home to the public arena.[2] Homemakers vary enormously in the extent to which they are cloistered and apolitical. As with most stereotypes, there is but a kernel of truth in depicting them as isolated and sheltered. They carry on transactions outside the home frequently, if not daily, and many are active in voluntary organizations that take them out of the private sphere. We will see in the data reported here that even a decade ago only 30 percent of the homemakers in a national sample of Americans were completely without organizational life in the community. Homemakers are a heterogeneous lot, different on average from employed women but not of one mind. Some are as active as employed women in political activities, some more so.[3]

Still, while public and private spheres should be viewed in relative terms, the greater participation of men in the public and of women in the private

2. Indeed, in the distinction between public and private that first emerged in ancient Greece, work and economic life were part of the private sphere—the household governed by necessity (Arendt, 1958).

3. College-educated, married mothers, especially those whose husbands hold high-status jobs, have traditionally been active participants in politics (McDonagh, 1982). It is only among single mothers, whose time, energy, and financial resources are scarce, that motherhood appears to depress participation (Sapiro, 1983).

captures a genuine difference in their social experiences. But how might these differences be conceptualized? In addition to different value emphases, what properties of the public and private spheres might foster and inhibit political engagement? I suggest below that differences in the social structures of the two spheres are what influence political thinking as well as activity and inactivity.

Social Structures of the Private and Public Spheres

Individuals in modern societies hold a large number of statuses. In Robert Merton's (1968) language, these are defined as the individual's *status set*, the complement of statuses in which the individual finds herself: wife, mother, worker, union member, Democrat, neighbor, PTA member, president of the block club, and so on. Many analysts use the concept of *multiple roles* instead of status set. Peter Blau (1975) notes that the concept of multiple roles directs attention to the ways individuals cope with diverse demands made on them by various statuses, while the concept of status set directs attention to the dimensions on which social positions are distinguished and the consequent multiplicity of statuses that characterize the social structure.

Some statuses facilitate the acquisition of new statuses while others retard it. For example, the status of paid worker tends to lead to membership in a professional organization or union. Some work statuses within a national or multinational company lead not only to additional statuses but also to cosmopolitan experiences and exposure to widely divergent perspectives. In contrast, the status of mother has historically precluded many statuses; even when it did lead to additional statuses, they were nearly always located in the local environment.

Some statuses also include more complex role sets. A *role set* is the complement of role relationships a person has by virtue of occupying a particular social status (Merton, 1968). In the status of candidate for political office, the role set includes constituents, party members, the other party's contender for the same office, the media, one's staff, other office holders, and doubtless many others. These role partners may conflict in their demands for allegiance and their expectations of the candidate. In this sense, the status of candidate encompasses a complex role set.

Rose Coser (1975) develops the distinction between simple and complex role sets. A simple (or restricted) role set includes only a few role partners who do not differ much in status positions or perspectives. They rarely change and are thoroughly familiar to the status occupant, as in a family or *gemeinschaft*. A complex role set is larger and more diverse with respect to the partners' statuses, ranks, and points of view, and it includes novelty and instability. Role partners tend to come and go and are not so familiar to the status occupant.

With one exception, these differences between simple and complex role sets correspond to those that in political theory distinguish the private from the public sphere. For Hannah Arendt, whose identification of the public and political derives from Aristotle, the public is characterized by relations among diverse peers and is governed by freedom, the private governed by necessity, by relations of domination among people with similar views (Pitkin, 1981). Although this emphasis on equality (and the reciprocity that it produces)[4] contrasts with Coser's stress on hierarchy, these treatments of public life and complex role sets are otherwise quite similar. In particular, they share a conviction that diversity in the perspectives of others will simultaneously advance action and democracy, on the one hand, and individuality and freedom, on the other.

The public sphere can thus be described as a social structure in which individuals tend to have large, interconnected status sets, many of which are also defined structurally by complex role sets. The private sphere involves a relatively simple social structure. Differences in the social structures (as well as values) of the two spheres give women unequal psychological and organizational resources for becoming politically active and developing consciousness of gender inequities in society.

I focus on two sets of examples: the status of worker compared to that of homemaker, and the statuses of the nontraditional and traditional participants in community affairs. Women who work in the paid labor force and homemakers who assume nontraditional volunteer statuses function in the public sphere not simply because these statuses take them outside the home. Rather, the women exist in the public sphere by virtue of the structural properties of the statuses. In contrast, women who stay cloistered in the home and even those who participate in the community in traditionally female activities, are situated in a less complex social structure.

4. This is not an unimportant difference since equality in relationships is considered critical to role-taking by many psychologists. Piaget (1948) and psychologists influenced by him argue, for example, that children need peers because it is only with equals that reciprocity and conflict occur. And when children play games and argue with others as equals, they have to think about how they would play the other person's part in the game and how the other person may behave and what she or he may think. When children interact with parents or teachers or more prestigious children, they do not engage in as much role-taking and tend instead to accept or ignore what the superordinate person says. The argument developed here is that complex social structures will foster understanding of social arrangements.

How is the worker status more complex than that of homemaker? Generally, it includes numerous role partners who hold statuses in many different levels of the organizational hierarchy. The worker's role set includes equals, subordinates, superordinates, and partners with diverse expectations of the individual worker as well as diverse perspectives on labor, management, and other organizational issues. The homemaker status usually includes fewer role partners who are also more similar to one another. The role sets of homemakers and workers, moreover, differ in their novelty and instability. New role partners—for example, newly dependent parents, additional children, adult children returning to the home—do enter the lives of homemakers, but this happens on average less often than new role partners come and go in the world of work.

Some community participant statuses also involve more complex role sets than others. This is true in two senses. First, some volunteer statuses are basically extensions of the homemaker status. Volunteering at a child's school, taking a leadership position in the PTA, serving on the board of a family social agency, or participating in social clubs comprised largely of other homemakers can be viewed this way. Although the role partners are not the same individuals as those within the family, their expectations and perspectives tend to reinforce rather than contradict those expressed by the role set associated with homemaker. Second, the role sets associated with these kinds of volunteer statuses include partners who are themselves similar in status, rank, and perspectives, and often they are also all women. In these ways, such statuses are traditional for homemakers, despite their physical location outside the home. In contrast, volunteering on commissions of local governments, becoming involved in local political controversies over pollution or the placement of industrial plants or shopping malls, or participating in block organizations puts homemakers into statuses that press them to think about matters beyond the well-being of their own family and children. Belonging to organizations that do not focus exclusively on the family adds discordancy, not just multiplicity, to the social relationships of the homemaker. These nontraditional statuses are also structured with greater complexity in that the role partners change more often and are more diverse with respect to gender, status, rank, and perspectives.

Implications of the Structural Properties of Statuses

How might the structural properties of particular statuses promote political consciousness and activity among women? I emphasize the structural contrast between the status of paid worker and homemaker, suggesting specific ways that these structural properties influence the different components of gender consciousness. Their impact on political activity is suggested in discussing the action component of consciousness.

The status of paid worker. The larger, interconnected status sets and more complex role sets associated with working should influence all aspects of gender consciousness. First I discuss how employment might foster identification. Since role sets at work encompass diverse and sometimes contradictory points of view, working women are assisted in grasping the significance of groups and categories. They learn that others in the role set disagree, not just as individuals, but as representatives of different categories and positions in the organization. They begin to understand the concept of group interests and the difference between the private opinion of an individual and the stance he or she expresses in a public role or on behalf of particular categories of workers. To function within complex role sets, workers have to think about groups and categories.

Second, work experience also gives women new information about gender relationships that should foster collective discontent. The extensive segregation and wage disparity in the labor market show them that gender is a significant basis of differentiation. While some working women do not perceive that men and women are channeled into different jobs and that women earn less than men, information about these matters is far more available to them than to homemakers. And categorical treatment is perceived more readily in settings where performance is supposed to predominate over ascriptive bases of differentiation. Since allusions to gender are normatively more appropriate in the homemaker status, they strike a less discordant note. Some discordance may be necessary to recognize that an individual is being treated categorically rather than individually, since the very idea of categorical treatment contradicts cultural patterns and individualistic biases in causal thinking. Gender in particular is so much taken for granted that it is difficult to perceive that men and women are treated differently (Bem and Bem, 1970).

The individual woman worker may draw her own conclusions about disparity, perhaps from being treated categorically herself or from observing differences in the treatment of other women relative to men. Role partners and networks at work, however, can abbreviate the task of seeking information and drawing inferences individually. Women's caucuses, unions, and professional associations as well as informal discussions and casual conversations provide working women with information that is not readily available to more socially isolated individuals except as they set out to study organizations and society. Since these networks disseminate information about the distribution of jobs, benefits, wages, and working conditions of men and women, recognition of categorical treatment does not have to emerge as just an individual interpretation of experience.

Cloistered homemakers and even those who take part in traditional community activities encounter fewer opportunities for perceiving gender as a basis for categorical treatment. If anything, their social experiences encourage them to take traditional gender arrangements for granted. Since their role sets include fewer role partners who are also more homogeneous in outlook, they have fewer structural pressures and opportunities for thinking about categories and groups. They also lack the direct experience of observing men and women in the marketplace. Labor-market disparities have to be understood abstractly, if at all.

The social networks of homemakers cannot compensate entirely for these structural limitations. These networks, especially for homemakers who have young children, are relatively limited in scope and character (Flora and Lynn, 1974; Lynn and Flora, 1973). Homemakers on average are embedded in fewer networks than married women who work (Sapiro, 1983). Their networks, largely set in the neighborhood, do not possess as much social knowledge about gender disparities in the public arena and tend to avoid controversial and political conversations in order to maintain their intensity and stability (Lopata, 1971). Therefore, even when the role sets of homemakers include varied perspectives, conflict, and potential controversy, pressures against political discussion and limited information about disparity militate against homemakers' becoming aware of categorical treatment.

Third, employed women are also stimulated to question the legitimacy of gender disparities, since the diversity of their role sets fosters sensitivity to social causation. The individual more easily discovers that when there are several contradictory expectations in the role set, conflict lies in the social situation, not between the self and others (Merton, 1968). The structure of the worker's role set thus potentially counters the "fundamental attribution bias" (Nisbett and Ross, 1980). A shift from individual to structural, external explanations is at the heart of the legitimacy issue. Wage disparity between men and women will not be judged as illegitimate if women believe it arises mostly from the deficiences of individual female workers or from the special talents of male workers. Raising questions about legitimacy thus requires thinking about causation in ways that counter fundamental cognitive biases. Although the complexity of role sets at work will not automatically check these biases, the kind of information made available and discussed in social networks at work has a good chance of doing so. It is consensus information that emphasizes the commonality of women's work experiences. Information that highlights commonality and prevalence helps people appreciate the importance of social circumstances (Kelley, 1972). Learning that women commonly earn less than men encourages women to consider structural explanations of wage disparity that they might otherwise attribute entirely to differences in the talents of a particular man and woman. This social learning, abetted by the role sets and social networks at work, is less available to homemakers.

The unfamiliarity and instability characteristic of complex role sets at work also induce active, reflective thought. Since role partners come and go and at times present unexpected demands, they goad the working woman to think and reflect on the social world. An active, reflective style is a resource for considering the significance of gender in society, just as it is for understanding other features of society. When role partners are more familiar and stable, as they more often are in the homemaker status, the woman already knows what they think and feel. She does not have to work so hard to articulate her role in relation to others (Coser, 1975) and does not have to think as much about the social world. Moreover, the impact of the greater familiarity and stability of the homemaker's role set is not on thought alone. Familiar, stable role sets also mitigate against change, because role partners in these long-standing relationships generally are emotionally invested in stability. To be free to change, adults often have to leave familiar and stable networks (Wilcox, 1981).

Fourth, homemakers and workers also possess unequal resources for forming collective orientations, working on behalf of other women and becoming involved in the broader political arena. Organizational bases in the world of work reduce time and personal energy demands that would be required from the individual were she to act on her own. Organizational resources thus increase the likelihood that women will organize to change the conditions or policies they believe constrain women's lives and that they will find ways to translate their political awareness of gender issues into a broader political agenda in electoral politics. The ease of action offered by unions, professional associations, and women's caucuses is far greater than that of individuals who must act alone and privately, if at all. Of course, working women have less free time for politics, but this cost is more than offset by the organizational resources.

All in all, the complexity of the role sets associated with work provide a training ground for political action. Women learn that controversy is ubiquitous. Experience in worker organizations, either union or management, or in special interest groups on the job teaches political skills and counteracts the values and personal styles ascribed to the private sphere. Political skills include analyzing situations, developing strategies, bargaining, and forming liaisons. Of course, some job settings offer more opportunities than others to learn these skills and to take part in political action, and some workers are more engaged than others. Still, the opportunities working women have to become politically knowledgeable, skilled, and active typically exceed those of homemakers. At a minimum, chances to observe political processes first hand are greater in the labor market than at home. These organizational resources should encourage involvement not only in activities aimed at the work institution itself but even in those concerned with local and national electoral politics.

Overcoming inhibitors to gender consciousness. The import of structural resources and constraints is sharpened by considering some of the cultural and psychological forces that tend to discourage group identification and inhibit perception of group-based inequities. To identify with a social category and feel aggrieved about its treatment, one must first become aware that categories exist and sometimes influence how individuals fare economically and socially. This appreciation of the significance of categories is in some ways antithetical to prevailing cultural values in industrialized liberal democracies. Ascriptive criteria, family origin, and group membership are not supposed to determine, or even heavily influence, the success or failure of the individual. One's group membership is generally considered less influential and is valued less than one's unique qualities. In general, Americans do not like to categorize themselves; they prefer to think of themselves merely as individuals. Individual distinctiveness is valued; similarities to others who share the same demographic features are not (Snyder and Fromkin, 1980).

Although culturally implanted, our reluctance to identify with categories and to think categorically also has cognitive and emotional roots. We tend to prefer vivid, concrete information over statistics and distributional information; yet, we need statistics to compare categories and evaluate differences between them. Recent research demonstrates that many people do not fully understand or use statistical heuristics such as base rates, sample bias, and the law of large numbers (Nisbett and Ross, 1980).[5] Not comfort-

5. There are some conditions under which people do seem to understand and apply statistics better than has been commonly thought. Use of statistical heuristics increases when people believe that the population is heterogeneous, when the role of chance is made salient to them, when they have experience and familiarity with the events, when the culture specifies statistical reasoning as normative, and when they are trained in the use of statistics (Nisbett et al., 1983). However, a close look at the proportions in these studies shows that, even under optimal conditions, only about half of the subjects show statistical competence.

able with distributional phenomena, many people fall back on their knowledge of the individual case and counter statistical conclusions with anecdotes or exceptions that invalidate the central tendency.

Causal inference is also biased individualistically. Cause is attributed unduly to individual rather than social circumstances. Social circumstances need to be prominent and incontrovertibly significant to force recognition of commonality and common cause (Nisbett and Ross, 1980). Moreover, even when individuals are able to perceive commonalities and categorical distinctions, they don't necessarily apply them to their own lives. For example, while a large proportion of blacks and women know that race and sex discrimination occur in the society at large, many fewer believe that they have personally experienced it. Faye Crosby (1984) discusses several reasons for this selective vision: individuals have difficulty obtaining and interpreting information about their personal cases, they feel angry and helpless when they have to consider themselves as victims, and they need to believe in a just world.

Certain societal characteristics of the United States further discourage individuals from becoming group-conscious. During most of its history, the United States has been characterized by an expanding economy, high rates of geographical shifts in population, and enough intergenerational mobility that Americans, aided by the ideology of individualism and meritocracy, have perceived even more status change than has actually existed. These conditions all encourage individualistic thinking and discourage recognition of group disparities or awareness of structural forces that may impede the achievements of certain categories.

There are theoretical grounds for supposing that women should develop group consciousness even less easily than members of other subordinate categories in America. Women lack many of the structural conditions that usually promote group consciousness (Merton, 1968; Williams, 1975; Tajfel, 1978; Williams and Giles, 1978). Awareness of inequality is facilitated when the stratification system produces large and dramatic differences between social categories. Gender inequality, while marked and doggedly persistent with respect to wages, is not as extreme as racial inequality and it is also lower in the United States than in most other Western industrialized nations. Data from eight nations—the United States, Finland, Switzerland, the Netherlands, Great Britain, Italy, Germany, and Austria—indicate that the smallest gender gaps in personal income are in the United States and Finland (Jennings and Farah, 1980), while gender inequality is most pronounced in Germany and Austria.

More important, the structure of gender relations inhibits the growth of gender consciousness among women. Solidarity and recognition of group deprivation are fostered when members of a category interact frequently with each other and only occasionally with members of the outgroup; when intimate interaction is restricted to the ingroup; and when relations with members of the outgroup are conflictual (Coser, 1956), predominantly competitive, or, at the very least, not intimate (Billig, 1976; Stephan, 1985; Tajfel, 1978; Williams, 1975). The structure of gender relations could not be more different from this pattern. Women have both frequent and intimate relations with men. Men and women also share economic gains and losses as members of families. For many women, associations outside the family involve crosscutting ties, both with men and with more privileged women, that keep them from perceiving the deprived circumstances of women as a class (Coser, 1956; Deschamps and Doise, 1978; Merton, 1968).

Given these cultural, psychological, and social impediments, it is not surprising that women tend not to be as politically conscious of their subordination as are other subordinate categories in America. The relative weakness of women's gender consciousness is demonstrated in two ways in analyses my colleagues and I have carried out. Except for their strong critique of the legitimacy of gender disparities in the labor market, women's political consciousness is weaker than that of blacks, the elderly, and blue-collar workers. Moreover, women do not express a distinctively subordinate consciousness—they share views very similar to men's about the position of women in society. This consensus contrasts dramatically with the subordinate-superordinate polarization of the perspectives of blacks and whites (Gurin, Miller, and Gurin, 1980; Gurin, 1985).

Of course, women vary greatly. The lives of some women put them in structural conditions that tend to counteract and sometimes overcome these impediments to gender consciousness. The lives of other women keep them in constraining social structures. It is to these subgroup differences that we turn now.

Multiplicity and Particular Statuses

To examine the statuses that might foster women's gender consciousness and participation in electoral politics, I analyzed data collected in three national surveys conducted at the Institute for Social Research, the University of Michigan: the 1972 and 1976 national election studies (NES) and two waves of the monthly consumer surveys in 1983.[6]

Let us look first at the relative importance of multiple statuses and the particular statuses adult women hold. We focus on three: spouse vs. non-

6. Individuals interviewed in the 1972 and 1976 national election surveys were a representative cross-section of U.S. citizens eighteen years of age or older who were living in private

spouse; parent vs. nonparent; and paid worker vs. homemaker. Since two of the surveys—the 1976 NES and 1983 consumer survey—included identical questions about these statuses, replicability of results could be checked.

Definition of the Status Groups

Respondents in the surveys were asked to define themselves as employed, unemployed, disabled, retired, homemakers, or students. Homemakers were also asked if they had worked for pay, including part-time, during the year preceding the survey. In order to study the impact of current statuses of paid worker and homemaker, I deleted from the analysis (1) women who had worked for pay earlier in their lives but were at the time of the survey retired, disabled, or unemployed, and (2) students. Also, because I wanted a clean distinction between currently employed women and homemakers, I deleted women who defined themselves as homemakers but who had worked part-time during the preceding year. Respondents were asked if they were married, separated, divorced, widowed, or single and listed their children by age. In order to focus on current statuses, I deleted from the analysis women who were not currently involved in parenting since *all* their children were eighteen years of age or older.[7]

The women included in the analysis were defined by three dimensions. The first was marital status, divided into those currently married and those not married (separated, divorced, single, or widowed); next, parental status, with mothers of at least one child younger than eighteen, and nonmothers;[8] finally, employment status, including currently employed women and homemakers who had not worked for pay during the preceding year. Table 12.1 shows the number of women in each of these status groups in 1976 and 1983.

Measures of Gender Consciousness and Electoral Participation

Measures of the four dimensions of gender consciousness were collected in both surveys. In addition, the 1976 survey asked questions about voting in the presidential election and participation in electoral politics.

---

households in the coterminous United States. The interviews were collected face-to-face. Individuals interviewed in the 1983 survey were also a representative cross-section of persons eighteen years of age or older. These interviews were collected by telephone.

7. In 1976, 252 women were deleted because they were not currently employed, 63 because they were homemakers who had worked part-time the preceding year, and 280 because all their children were eighteen or older. This left 716 women who met the criteria for inclusion. In 1983, 153 women were deleted because they were not currently employed, 69 because they were homemakers working part-time, and 30 because they did not answer the question about children living at home. This left 485 women.

8. In 1983, respondents were asked only if they had any children eighteen years or younger still living at home but not to list their children by age. This means that some of the nonmothers in the 1983 sample may in fact have been parents whose children were all older than eighteen.

Table 12.1: Classification of Samples by Work, Marriage, and Parental Status

| | 1976 N = 716 | | | | 1983 N = 485 | | | |
| | Currently Employed N = 428 | | Nonworking Homemakers N = 288 | | Currently Employed N = 366 | | Nonworking Homemakers N = 119 | |
	Not married	Married	Not married	Married	Not married	Married	Not married	Married
Parent of child younger than 18	72	175	56	195	68	93	26	65
Nonparent[+]	115	66	6	31	114	91	2	26

[+] Nonparents in 1983 include some women whose children are eighteen or older. This accounts for the larger proportion of the 1983 sample in that category. The 1976 results are thus based on the more accurate distinction between parents and nonparents.

Identification was measured differently in 1976 and 1983. In 1976, respondents were asked to judge how similar they were to a set of sixteen social categories, including "women." They were asked to pick all the category labels to which they felt close—that is, those categories composed of people who "are most like you in their ideas and interests and feelings about things." Then they were asked to pick a category to which they felt closest. Women who did not pick the label "women" as a category to which they felt close were described as "not identified." "Identified" women said they felt close but not closest to the category "women"; and "closely identified" women said they felt closest to that category. In 1983, women were asked about their sense of common fate—that is, the extent to which they believed that "what happens to women generally in this country will have something to do with what happens in your life." Women who perceived no common fate or not very much were "not identified"; women who perceived some were "identified"; and women who perceived a lot were "strongly-identified."[9]

Collective discontent was measured from evaluations of the influence of various groups in American society. The interviewer stated: "Some people think that certain groups have too much influence in American life and politics, while other people feel that certain groups don't have as much influence as they deserve." As the interviewer read the category labels, including "women" and "men," respondents judged whether the category had "too much influence," "just about the right amount," or "too little influence." Collective discontent is the judgement that, relative to men, women have less influence than they deserve.

Two evaluations of *illegitimacy* were measured. First, the illegitimacy of traditional gender roles was operationalized by asking respondents to place themselves on a seven-point scale, where 7 represented illegitimacy ("men and women should have an equal role in running business, industry, and government") and 1 indicated legitimacy ("a woman's place is in the home"). Second, the illegitimacy of market disparities was measured by asking respondents to explain the causes of gender differences in income

9. Other analyses that my colleagues and I have carried out demonstrate that identification defined as a sense of common fate is more closely related to other components of gender consciousness than is perceived similarity (Gurin and Townsend, 1986). The relative importance of perceived similarity and sense of common fate to subjective group membership has long been controversial. Many years ago Lewin (1948) argued that people become, and feel themselves to be, a group because they share interdependence of fate, not because they are similar to each other. Here I am not concerned with their relative importance but with the impact of women's statuses on each.

and occupational status. In 1976, these explanations were presented as forced-choice alternatives, attributed either to institutional arrangements such as discrimination, poor schooling, or seniority; or to women's personal deficiencies such as lack of ambition or to tastes and preferences antithetical to market success. Choosing the structural over the personal attribution was taken as evidence that the woman was critical of legitimacy. Of course, the forced-choice method makes it difficult to determine if the respondent's criticism was based more on recognizing structural causes or on rejecting the causal significance of gender differences in endowments and preferences. In 1983, the statements attributing market disparities to personal differences between men and women were presented as Likert-type scales on which respondents could disagree strongly or somewhat, agree strongly or somewhat. Scores can be interpreted clearly: illegitimacy means that women rejected the claim that market inequalities are the fair result of the unequal endowments of men and women.

Collective orientation was also measured in two ways. One question assessed attitude toward the label "women's liberation movement" on a feeling thermometer. Respondents were told that thermometer readings of 0 to 49 represented a cold or unfavorable feeling, 50 a neutral feeling, and 51 to 100, warm or favorable. The second was a two-item index comprised of forced-choice questions in which one alternative advocated that women should work together to change conditions affecting the group as a whole, the other that each woman should act individually in her own behalf.

Electoral participation was measured in 1976 but not in 1983. One indicator of participation was the respondent's self-report as to whether she voted in the 1976 presidential election. The other was an index summarizing whether she had tried to influence someone else's vote, worked for a political party, attended a political meeting, been a member of a political organization other than a party, displayed a campaign button or sticker, or contributed money to a candidate during the 1976 campaign.

Number of Statuses

The question of interest is whether multiplicity of statuses or a particular kind of status produces greater political involvement and gender consciousness. Table 12.2 summarizes the 1976 and 1983 effects of number of statuses, marriage, motherhood, and paid employment. It shows clearly that multiplicity itself was not important in either year. There is simply no evidence here that a multiple-status lifestyle influences either gender consciousness or participation in electoral politics.

When I examined the means of the eight groups of women, it was obvious

Table 12.2: Effects of Number of Statuses and Three Particular Statuses on Gender Consciousness and Electorial Participation

	1976 N = 716						1983 N = 485					
	Number of statuses	Marriage Entire sample	Marriage Among employed	Parenthood Entire sample	Parenthood Among employed	Employment	Number of statuses	Marriage Entire sample	Marriage Among employed	Parenthood Entire sample	Parenthood Among employed	Employment
Gender Consciousness												
Collective Discontent	NS	**	NS	*	NS	***	NS	**	NS	NS	NS	****
Reject Legtimacy of:												
Traditional gender roles	NS	**	NS	*	NS	*****	NS	***	*	NS	NS	*****
Gender disparity in marketplace‡	NS	***	NS	' ***	*	*****	NS	NS	NS	NS	NS	****
Identification‡	NS	**	NS	*	NS	***	NS	***	*	NS	NS	****
Collective Orientation												
Approve women's liberation movement	NS	*	NS	*	NS	****	NS	**	NS	NS	NS	*****
Approve collective action	***	***	**	***	**	**	—	—	—	—	—	—
Electoral Participation												
Participate in campaign activities	NS	NS	NS	NS	NS	****	—	—	—	—	—	—
Voted in last election	NS	NS	NS	NS	NS	****	—	—	—	—	—	—

Note: NS = not significant.

‡ In 1976, measure was forced-choice; in 1983, a Likert-type measure.

‡ In 1976, identification was measured by asking for perceived similarity to other women; in 1983, it was measured by asking for extent of common fate with other women.

* .05   ** .01   *** .001   **** .0001   ***** < .0001

why multiplicity itself was insignificant. In the first place, there were almost no adult women without at least one of these statuses, and a majority of those with only one status were single, childless, and employed. Their employment gave them a positive political advantage. The average gender consciousness and participation scores of women with only one status were thus quite high. Second, the average scores of women with two statuses were low, especially in 1976, because a majority of them were nonemployed married mothers who expressed unusually traditional views of gender relations. These two groups of women—those whose one status was employment and those whose joint statuses were marriage and motherhood—largely explain why there was no effect of multiplicity itself.

Table 12.2 also shows the effects of each of the three statuses. The effects on gender consciousness of marriage, significant in both years, and motherhood, significant in 1976, were largely spurious. Unmarried women and nonparents appeared to be more politically conscious, but this was actually attributable to their higher employment rate. In 1976, 24 percent more unmarried than married women (20 percent more in 1983) were employed. When employment was controlled and the effect of marriage was examined just among employed women, marriage was no longer a significant negative influence on most components of gender consciousness. Similarly, the negative effect of motherhood in 1976 disappeared when employment was controlled (table 12.2).

The Worker and Homemaker Statuses

As predicted, the status of paid worker was consistently related to gender consciousness and participation in electoral politics. Compared to homemakers who did not work at all outside the home, employed women were more strongly identified with other women, discontented over women's lack of power relative to men, critical of traditional gender roles and the legitimacy of market disparities, and collectively oriented. This was true in both 1976 and 1983. They were also more involved in campaign activities in the 1976 election and more frequently voted in that election.

To some extent, this effect of employment is exaggerated since employed women were also younger and better educated. In 1976, they were approximately five years younger than homemakers, and 13 percent more of them reported some college education. In 1983, the youth and schooling edges of the employed women were nearly identical to those of 1976. This is important since women with more schooling were also more politically conscious and active in politics; younger women also exhibited stronger gender consciousness (although age was not a significant determinant of political participation).[10] Therefore, part of the reason employed women were more politically conscious and active in electoral politics is that they possessed more personal resources for political life.

Does employment still influence gender consciousness and political activity after adjusting for these personal resources? Table 12.3 presents the size of the unadjusted effect of employment and the standardized regression coefficients for employment after adjusting for age, years of schooling, marital status, and motherhood. Even controlling their resources, employed women were still significantly more gender conscious on nearly all measures; they were also more politically active. The effect of employment was reliable and robust in both 1976 and 1983.

Cloistered, Traditional, and Nontraditional Homemakers

The data collected in the 1972 national election survey were used to explore a different, largely unexamined issue—the importance of multiple and particular statuses of homemakers. Homemakers are exceedingly varied. Apart from the commonality that they do not work in the paid labor force, they differ enormously. Some are mothers, some not. Some are active in the community, some not. The volunteer statuses of some basically extend and reinforce their homemaker statuses by focusing on the well-being of family and children. Other volunteer statuses press homemakers to consider broader community problems and put them into more complex social structures.

The 1972 NES asked questions about organizations and community involvements. This made it possible for us to examine the impact of performing in multiple statuses—being both a homemaker *and* a participant in community life outside the home—and of particular statuses: being a cloistered homemaker, a traditional community participant, and a nontraditional community participant. The interviewer said: "Here is a list of some kinds of organizations to which people may belong. Just tell me any that you belong to. If you belong to any that are not on this list, tell me about those, too." Later the interviewer asked respondents who had school-age children if they took part in groups that try to improve the quality of schools in their communities.

Organizations were classified as *traditional* extensions of the homemaker role if they seemed concerned primarily with the welfare of children

---

10. In 1976, correlations of education with political participation ranged from .28 to.35 and, with gender consciousness, .05 to .35. In 1983, education again correlated with gender consciousness, .09 to .39 across the different indicators. In 1976, the age correlations with gender consciousness ranged from .02 to -.31, and, in 1983, from -.02 to -.33.

Table 12.3: *Effect of Employment on Gender Consciousness and*
Participation in Electoral Politics
(Standard errors in parentheses)

	1976 N = 716		1983 N = 485	
	Unadjusted effect	Beta, adjusted for age, years of school, marriage, parenthood	Unadjusted effect	Beta, adjusted for age, years of school, marriage, parenthood
Gender Consciousness				
Collective Discontent	.128***	.063** (.026)	.169****	.126**** (.036)
Reject Legitimacy of:				
Traditional gender roles	.228*****	.143**** (.026)	.259*****	.201***** (.034)
Gender disparity in marketplace[+]	.205*****	.141**** (.027)	.123****	.043 (NS) (.034)
Identification[+]	.111***	.060* (.026)	.186****	.116*** (.035)
Collective Orientation				
Approve women's liberation movement	.136****	.125*** (.028)	.228*****	.194**** (.037)
Approve collective action	.099**	.087** (.028)	—	—
Electoral Participation				
Participate in campaign activities	.141****	.091** (.026)	—	—
Voted in last election	.135****	.102** (.026)	—	—

[+] In 1976, measure was forced-choice; in 1983, a Likert-type measure.

[+] In 1976, identification was measured by asking for perceived similarity to other women; in 1983, it was measured by asking for extent of common fate with other women.

* .05 ** .01 *** .001 **** .0001 ***** < .0001

(PTAS, school improvement groups); nurturing and well-being of the family and the needy (charity or social welfare organizations); responsibility for morality and spirituality (religious groups beyond attending services); or sociability (card-playing groups, social clubs, fraternal lodges, or sororities). They were classified as *nontraditional* if they seemed concerned with the broader welfare of the community and issues beyond the family—for example, professional associations or unions; civic groups or government commissions; political clubs; special-interest groups or lobbies; ethnic, racial, or nationality associations; cooperatives.

On the basis of this information, I categorized three groups of homemakers: cloistered homemakers, the 30 percent who did not participate in any organization; traditional community participants, the 43 percent who were not sheltered in the private sphere but participated *only* in traditional extensions of the homemaker status; and nontraditional community participants, the 17 percent who were involved in at least one nontraditional organization. This third group nearly always participated in traditional organizations as well.

With one exception, the 1972 survey included the same measures of gender consciousness that have been previously described. In 1972, the collective discontent measure was phrased absolutely, not relatively: respondents were asked to judge only the influence of women in American life and politics. In addition, a third indicator of the legitimacy of disparity was included: respondents were asked if the first workers to be laid off should be women whose husbands have jobs or whether male and female employees should be treated the same way when a company has to lay off part of its labor force. Of course, the 1972 NES also included the same measures of voting and campaign activities that were asked in 1976.

The analysis of the gender consciousness of these three groups of homemakers demonstrates that it is not multiple statuses per se that encourage women to become politically conscious of gender disparities in the political and economic arenas. This is seen by comparing cloistered homemakers with the other two groups of homemakers, each of whom has added the status of community participant to that of homemaker (table 12.4). On none of the measures of gender consciousness were the cloistered homemakers significantly different from the combination of the two groups of community participants.

In contrast, particular statuses of these homemakers were related to gender consciousness. Nontraditional community participants were somewhat more critical of the legitimacy of traditional gender roles and of labor-market disparities between women and men. They were more iden-

Table 12.4: Gender Consciousness of Three Groups of Homemakers and Employed Women (1972)

	Cloistered homemakers (1)	Homemakers involved in traditional community activities (2)	Homemakers involved in nontraditional community activities (3)	Employed women (4)	Contrasts			
					Homemakers: number of statuses (1 vs. 2, 3)	Homemakers: type of status (3 vs. 1, 2)	Employed vs. all homemakers (1 to 3 vs. 4)	Employed vs. nontraditional homemakers (3 vs. 4)
	N = 146	N = 259	N = 84	N = 484				
Gender Consciousness								
Collective Discontent+ (Range 1–3)	2.23	2.20	2.44	2.45	NS	p = .06	p = .003	NS
Reject Legitimacy of:								
Traditional gender roles (Range 1–7)	2.79	2.80	3.41	3.98	NS	p = .08	p = .0000	p = .001
Gender disparity in marketplace (Range 1–5)	2.61	2.62	2.94	3.20	NS	p = .05	p = .0000	p = .004
Firing women first (Range 1–2)	1.34	1.36	1.49	1.60	NS	p = .05	p = .0000	p = .06
Identification (Range 1–3)	2.45	2.50	2.61	2.64	NS	p = .05	p = .0000	NS
Collective Orientation								
Approve women's liberation movement (Range 1–100)	52.97	53.04	53.46	54.74	NS	NS	NS	NS
Approve collective action (Range 1–3)	1.53	1.58	1.60	1.69	NS	NS	NS	NS
Electoral Participation								
Participate in campaign activities (Range 1–6)	1.24	1.43	1.69	1.62	p = .0007	p = .001	p = .001	NS
Voted in 1972 election (Range 1–5)	1.96	2.74	3.43	3.06	p = .0000	p = .0000	p = .003	NS

+ In 1972, collective discontent was measured only by asking for evaluations of the power of women.
For all measures, a higher score means more (e.g., discontent; stronger collective orientation).
NS means no statistically significant results appeared in contrasts.

tified with other women and more discontented over women's lack of political influence. But there were also ways in which they were not more feminist in their beliefs. They were no more approving of collective strategies than were other homemakers.

The heightened identification, discontent, and criticism of legitimacy among this group of homemakers gain importance when compared to the perspectives of women who were employed in the paid labor force. Not surprisingly, employed women were more politically conscious on all our measures except attitude toward collective strategies. This replicates what we have already learned from the analyses of the 1976 and 1983 data. What is more interesting is that the nontraditional community participants scored midway between employed women and other homemakers on the measures of legitimacy. They were as identified as employed women and held virtually the same evaluations of the political influence of women. Participation in particular nonfamily and nonwork statuses provides yet another means by which women begin to question and criticize traditional gender relationships in society.

The stronger gender consciousness of the nontraditional homemakers results partially from personal characteristics that distinguish them from other homemakers. On average, they were six years younger than the cloistered and eight years younger than the traditional community participants. They had also attained more education. Slightly over a third of them had graduated from college, while only about 10 percent of the cloistered and 15 percent of the traditional group had. Adjusting for their age and education advantages decreased the size of the nontraditional homemaker effect, although the differences between them and other homemakers did not entirely disappear when controls were applied. Table 12.5 documents statistically the fact the nontraditional homemakers were still somewhat more identified, discontented, and critical of legitimacy.

The analysis of participation in electoral politics produced a somewhat different picture. Both multiplicity and particular statuses proved important. The cloistered homemakers voted least often and were the least active in campaign activities. Even the traditionally involved homemakers were significantly more engaged in electoral politics. The nontraditionally involved homemakers were the most active. All of the comparisons were statistically significant, and they persisted when education and age were controlled. Simply having another status beyond that of homemaker fosters political activity.

Particular community statuses also influenced electoral activity. A comparison between the political activity of the nontraditional community participants and that of employed women shows that the former voted and took part in campaign activities at least as frequently as women who worked for pay outside the home (table 12.4). As one of the organizations coded as nontraditional was a political group, the nontraditional home-makers increased engagement in politics might have been largely defini-tional and redundant. To examine this possibility, I deleted women who mentioned political groups from the category of nontraditional homemak-ers (a total of 19 of the 84 women) and compared those remaining to employed women. Even this subset of the nontraditional homemakers were as active as employed women in campaign activities, and also voted as frequently in the 1972 presidential election as the employed women.

Table 12.5: *Effect of Homemakers' Participation in Nontraditional Community Activities (1972)*

	Eta,[+] Nontraditional vs. all other homemakers	Beta,[+] Nontraditional vs. all other homemakers
Gender Consciousness		
Identification	.094*	.079*
Collective Discontent	.103*	.068 (p = .08)
Reject Legitimacy of:		
Traditional gender roles	.067 (p = .08)	.024
Gender disparity in marketplace	.087*	.064 (p = .08)
Firing women first	.092*	.081*
Electoral Participation		
Participate in campaign activities	.187***	.112***
Voted in 1972 election	.253****	.154***

[+] Eta shows the size of the difference between nontraditional and all other home-makers when no controls for personal resources for politics were applied. Beta shows the size of the difference after the relative youth and educational advan-tages of the nontraditional homemakers were controlled.
* .05   *** .001   **** .0001

In these analyses, we have unambiguously answered the question: Is it a multiple-status lifestyle or a particular kind of status that promotes gender consciousness? Multiplicity itself was unimportant. Instead, two particular statuses were influential. The status of paid worker fostered gender consciousness in 1972, 1976, and 1983, and its effect remained significant after adjusting for the relative youth and educational advantages of employed women. The status of nontraditional community participant provided a different but important route to feminist consciousness for nonemployed homemakers. Although nontraditional community participants represented a small portion of all homemakers, the impact of homemaking would have been misinterpreted had we not explored the ways in which their beliefs and attitudes deviated from those of cloistered and traditional homemakers. As these analyses demonstrate, women's lives are rich and varied, and there is more than one path to feminist consciousness.

Both of these statuses proved influential for participation in electoral politics. Employment, not number of statuses, was important in explaining turnout and campaign involvment in 1976. Employment was significant in 1972 as well, and among homemakers the status of nontraditional volunteer resulted in a rate of political participation equal to that of employed women. Whether women functioned *just* in the homemaker status or had a multiple-status lifestyle that included doing something in the community also had an effect. Compared to cloistered homemakers, even traditionally involved homemakers were more active politically, although less so than the nontraditional homemakers.

We see in these results that experience in the public sphere was an important influence in women's political thinking and action. But they also support the critics of the privatization explanation of women's relationship to politics. The extent of women's restriction to the private sphere is exaggerated in the contrast between homemakers and workers in the paid labor force. Most homemakers are *not* cloistered in the private sphere of domestic life. Many are engaged in community life; some are citizens in the sense meant by the ancient Greeks—participants in the polis acting to determine the collective good. Those homemakers whose community activities focused on collective rather than family life were fully engaged in the public sphere, and their enhanced gender consciousness and involvement in electoral politics confirmed it. Of course, the differentiation among homemakers that is drawn here in no way contradicts the significance of the private-public distinction, in that those women who were truly privatized showed the effects of this experience both in their acceptance of traditional conceptions of societal gender arrangements and in their lower turnout at the polls and participation in political campaigns.

Finally, the consistent support for the impact of the statuses of paid worker and nontraditional community participant gives indirect support for the structural hypothesis advanced in this paper. I have argued that it is the different social structures in the public and private spheres, along with their different values, that explain why employed women and nontraditional homemakers participate more actively in electoral politics and are more feminist in orientation, compared both to cloistered homemakers and to those who participate outside the home as an extension of the homemaker status. However, the multiplicity, diversity, instability, and novelty of the status- and role-sets of the three groups of homemakers and of employed women would need to be measured rather than inferred to subject the argument to a direct test. Such a test would also ideally check the theory's causal expectations, that adult experiences in the public sphere foster political thinking and action. The cross-sectional analyses reported here are moot on that point.

References

Andersen, K. (1975). Working women and political participation, 1952–1972. *American Journal of Political Science*, 19, 439–53.

Arendt, H. (1958). *The human condition*. Chicago: University of Chicago Press.

Barnes, S. H., and Kasse, M. (1979). *Political action: Mass participation in five Western democracies*. Beverly Hills: Sage.

Baxter, S., and Lansing, M. (1983). *Women and politics: The visible majority*. Ann Arbor: The University of Michigan Press.

Bem, S. L., and Bem, D. J. (1970). We're all unconscious sexists. *Psychology Today*, 4, 22–26, 115–16.

Billig, M. (1976). *Social psychology and intergroup relations*. London: Academic Press.

Blau, P. M. (1975). Structural constraints of status complements. In L. A. Coser (ed.) *The idea of social structure: Papers in honor of Robert K. Merton*. New York: Harcourt Brace Jovanovich.

Bourque, S. C., and Grossholtz, J. (1974). Politics as an unnatural practice: Political science looks at female participation. *Politics and Society*, 4, 225–66.

Christy, C. A. (1983). *Gender, employment, and political participation in eleven nations*. Paper presented at Annual Meeting of the American Political Science Association, The Palmer House, Chicago, September.

Commission of the European Communities (1984). *European men and women in 1983*. Brussels: Author.

Coser, L. A. (1956). *The functions of social conflict*. New York: Free Press.

Coser, R. L. (1975). The complexity of roles as a seedbed of individual autonomy. In L. A. Coser (ed.), *The idea of social structure: Papers in honor of Robert K. Merton*. New York: Harcourt Brace Jovanovich.

Crosby, F. J. (1982). *Relative deprivation and working women*. New York: Oxford University Press.

———. (1984). The denial of personal discrimination. *American Behavioral Scientist*, 27, 371–86.

Deschamps, J. C., and Doise, W. (1978). Crossed category memberships in intergroup relations. In H. Tajfel (ed.), *Differentiation between social groups*. New York: Academic Press.

Ferree, M. M. (1981). *Women's work and employment attitudes: A longitudinal causal model*. Paper presented at the American Sociological Association meeting, August.

Flora, C. B., and Lynn, N. B. (1974). Women and political socialization: Considerations of the impact of motherhood. In J. Jaquette (ed.), *Women in politics*. New York: Wiley.

Goot, M., and Reid, E. (1975). *Women and voting studies: Mindless matrons or sexist scientism?* Beverly Hills: Sage.

Gurin, P. (1985). Women's gender consciousness. *Public Opinion Quarterly*, 49, 143–63.

Gurin, P., Miller, H., and Gurin, G. (1980). Stratum identification and consciousness. *Social Psychology Quarterly*, 43, 30–47.

Gurin, P., Thornton, A., and O'Brien, K. (1985). Gender consciousness: The impact of status change. Unpublished Paper, New York: Russell Sage Foundation.

Gurin, P., and Townsend, A. (1986). Properties of gender identity and their implications for gender consciousness. *The British Journal of Social Psychology*, 25, 139–48.

Jennings, M. K. (1983). Gender Roles and inequalities in political participation: Results from an eight-nation study. *The Western Political Quarterly*, 36, 364–85.

Jennings, M. K., and Farah, B. G. (1980). *Gender and politics: Convergence or differentiation?* Paper presented at conference on political action, Bellagio, Italy, June.

Kelley, H. H. (1972). *Causal schemata and the attribution process*. Morristown, N. J.: General Learning Press.

Krauss, W. R. (1974). Political implications of gender roles: A review of the literature. *American Political Science Review*, 68, 1706–23.

Lewin, K. (1948). *Resolving social conflict*. New York: Harper.

Lopata, H. (1971). *Occupation: Housewife*. New York: Oxford.

Lynn, N. B., and Flora, C. B. (1973). Motherhood and political participation: The changing sense of self. *Journal of Political and Military Sociology*, Spring, 91–103.

Macke, A., Hudis, P. M., and Larrick, D. (1977). *Sex-role attitudes and employment among women: A dynamic model*. National Longitudinal Survey Conference, Washington, D. C., January.

McDonagh, E. L. (1982). To work or not to work: The differential impact of achieved and derived status upon the political participation of women, 1956–1976. *American Journal of Political Science*, 26, 280–97.

Merton, R. K. (1968). Continuities in the theory of reference group behavior. In R. K. Merton, *Social theory and social structure*. New York: Free Press.

Nisbett, R. E., Krantz, D. H., Jepson, C., and Kunda, Z. (1983). The use of statistical heuristics in everyday inductive reasoning. *Psychological Review*, 90, 339–63.

Nisbett, R. E., and Ross, L. (1980). *Human inference: Strategies and shortcomings*. Englewood Cliffs, N. J.: Prentice-Hall.

Orum, A. M., Cohen, R. S., Grasmuck, S., and Orum, A. W. (1974). Sex, socialization, and politics. *American Sociological Review*, 39, 197–209.

Piaget, J. (1948). *The moral judgement of the child*. Glencoe, Ill.: Free Press.

Pitkin, H. F. (1981). Justice: On relating private and public. *Political Theory*, 9, 327–52.

Rossi, A. S. (1980). Life-span theories and women's lives. *Signs: Journal of Women in Culture and Society*, 6, 4–32.

Sapiro, V. (1983). *The political integration of women: Roles, socialization, and politics*. Urbana: University of Illinois Press.

———. (1984). *What research on the political socialization of women can tell us about the political socialization of people*. Paper presented at Annual Meeting of the American Political Science Association, Washington, D. C., September.

Snyder, C. R., and Fromkin, H. L. (1980). *Uniqueness: The human pursuit of difference*. New York: Plenum Press.

Spitze, G. D. (1978). Role experiences of young women: A longitudinal test of the role hiatus hypothesis. *Journal of Marriage and the Family*, 40, 471–79.

Spitze, G. D., and Waite, L. J. (1980). Labor force and work attitudes: Young women's early experiences. *Sociology of Work and Occupations*, 7, 3–32.

Stephan, W. G. (1985). Intergroup relations. In G. Lindzey and E. Aronson (eds.), *The handbook of social psychology*. New York: Random House.

Tajfel, H. (1978). Social categorization, social identity, and social comparison. In H. Tajfel (ed.), *Differentiation between social groups*. New York: Academic Press.

Thornton, A., Alwin, D. F., and Camburn, D. (1983). Causes and consequences of sex-role attitudes and attitude change. *American Sociological Review*. 48, 211–27.

U.S. Bureau of the Census (1985). *Current Population Reports*, Series P–20, no. 397, January. Washington, D.C.: U.S. Government Printing Office.

Waldman, E. (1983). Labor force statistics from a family perspective. *Monthly Labor Review*, 106, 16–20.

Welch, S. (1977). Women as political animals? A test of some explanations for male-female political participation differences. *American Journal of Political Science*, 21, 711–30.

———. (1980). Sex differences in political activity in Britain. *Women and Politics*, 1, 29–46. Wilcox, D. L. (1981). Social support in adjusting to marital disruption: A network analysis. In B. H. Gottleib (ed.), *Social networks and social support*. Beverly Hills: Sage.

Williams, J., and Giles, H. (1978). The changing status of women in society: An intergroup perspective. In H. Tajfel (ed.), *Differentiation between social groups*. New York: Academic Press.

Williams, R. M., Jr. (1975). Relative deprivation. In L. A. Coser (ed.), *The idea of social structure: Papers in honor of Robert K. Merton*. New York: Harcourt Brace Jovanovich.

Contributors

Pamela K. Adelmann is a doctoral candidate in social psychology at the University of Michigan.

Toni C. Antonucci is Associate Research Scientist in Psychology at the Institute of Social Research at the University of Michigan.

Rosalind C. Barnett is a clinical psychologist and research associate at the Wellesley College Center for Research on Women.

Grace K. Baruch is Associate Director at the Wellesley College Center for Research on Women.

Lerita M. Coleman is Assistant Professor of Psychology at the University of Tennessee.

Faye J. Crosby is Professor of Psychology at Smith College.

Cynthia Fuchs Epstein is Professor of Sociology at the Graduate Center of the City University of New York and Resident Scholar at the Russell Sage Foundation.

Martha R. Fowlkes is Associate Professor and Associate Dean of the School of Family Studies at the University of Connecticut, Storrs.

Walter R. Gove is Professor of Sociology at Vanderbilt University.

Patricia Gurin is Professor of Psychology at the University of Michigan and Resident Scholar at the Russell Sage Foundation.

Janet E. Malley is a doctoral candidate in Boston University's Personality Program.

Janice M. Steil is Associate Professor of Psychology at the Derner Institute of Advanced Psychological Studies at Adelphi University.

Abigail J. Stewart is Associate Professor of Psychology at Boston University.

Peggy A. Thoits is Associate Professor of Sociology at Indiana University.

Beth A. Turetsky is a doctoral candidate in clinical psychology at the Derner Institute of Advanced Psychological Studies at Adelphi University.

Lois M. Verbrugge is Associate Research Scientist at the Institute of Gerontology at the University of Michigan.

Robert S. Weiss is Professor of Sociology and Director of the Work and Family Research Unit at the University of Massachusetts, Boston.

Carol Zeiss is a doctoral candidate in sociology at Vanderbilt University.